Gladly Will I Glory
In My Infirmities

"I have a group of intercessors in heaven to whom I speak asking them to intercede for me and those for whom I pray. They are my personal saints in heaven. Father Charles Kram has been a member of that group since he went home to God. In my mind and faith, he is already a saint in heaven."

    - **Monsignor Lawrence Stuebben**, retired priest of the Arch-
diocese of San Antonio

"Just observing and being around and listening to Fr. Kram, I was struck by the fact that he seemed to embody the very virtues that I found most lacking in myself. If he could be so strong in his life as he was, it certainly encouraged me to try harder in my life and circumstances."

    - **John Butschek**, personal friend of Father Kram

"Many holy people were a part of this great drama of a humble man afflicted with polio, his beloved parents who cared for him, and what God had in store for them. I am happy to have been a small part of this miracle."

    - **Most Reverend Charles V. Grahmann**, Bishop Emeritus
of Dallas

"Milo and I have read this wonderful summation of the life of Father Charles Kram. In reading this book, we came to know this remarkable and saintly man who turned adversity into a life of service to God. We believe this book is vital in the process of advancing sainthood for Father Kram."

    - **Marion G. Reamy**, author of *Flying Was My Destiny: The
True Flying Adventures of Hans Vandervlugt*, and her husband
Milo V. Reamy, pilot and flying enthusiast

"Very much enjoyed learning about the life of Fr. Charles Kram. He is a new intercessor to whom I can now turn. Thank you for writing this book."

    - **C. Niles**, editor

"We finished reading *Gladly Will I Glory In My Infirmities* and thoroughly enjoyed it. Thank you for sharing this story. We were completely captivated by Father Kram's life. Truly he was a very special priest."

    - **Jimmy and Pat Koranek**

Gladly Will I Glory In My Infirmities

A Joyful Journey Through Life
Despite Enormous Suffering

Anthony Warzecha

LEONINE PUBLISHERS
PHOENIX, ARIZONA

Published by Leonine Publishers LLC
Phoenix, Arizona
USA

ISBN-13: 978-1-942190-10-3

Printed in the United States of America
10 9 8 7 6 5 4 3 2 1

Library of Congress Control Number: 2015931316

Visit us online at www.leoninepublishers.com
For more information: info@leoninepublishers.com

Dedication

To Fr. Kram's caregivers (his parents, doctors, nurses, all other
hospital personnel, and friends—clergy and laity)
who lovingly and joyfully did for him all the things
he could not do for himself.

Prayer

"May love be always the first and finest reason for everything you do and may it continue to grow in your hearts. May many blessings come to you and may the Lord Jesus keep you close to his heart."

(Prayer Fr. Kram sent to students at a school in Houston on February 15, 2000, a few months before he died.)

Contents

Preface

Each one of us is a product of many factors, some of which we cannot control. For example, there is the matter of when we were born. Was it in the twentieth century or the twelfth? Either one has a bearing on how we live. There is the matter of where we were raised. Was it in the United States, and if so, was it in New York or Texas, and if it was in Texas, was it in Houston or Shiner? Wherever it was, it had a bearing on our lives.

There is, of course, the matter of our heritage. The culture in which we grew up naturally had a bearing on who and what we became.

Then, there are circumstances that just seem to happen. There are a few things in life that can be predicted and there are some that result from our choices and actions, but many come to us as surprises.

And then, there are certain happenings that are our destiny. There are certain happenings ordained by our Creator that will occur or will not occur depending on our exercise of the free will with which our Creator blessed us.

This is the story of many factors and many people who shaped the life of a remarkable man *as well as* the story of how that remarkable man shaped the lives of many people around him.

As you prepare to enter into this journey, pray that God will open your heart to the love that is so evident throughout this story.

CHAPTER ONE

Charles's Youth

In the Beginning

In the beginning, when God created the heavens and the earth, the earth was a formless wasteland, and darkness covered the abyss, while a mighty wind swept over the waters. (Genesis 1:1–2)

At the time when the Lord made the earth and the heavens, while as yet there was no field shrub on earth and no grass of the field had sprouted, for the Lord God had sent no rain upon the earth and there was no man to till the soil, but a stream was swelling up out of the earth and was watering the ground, the Lord God formed man out of the clay of the ground and blew into his nostrils the breath of life, and so man became a living being. (Genesis 2:4–7)

The Family

Holy Scripture reveals that God created mankind in his own image. In his great love and wisdom and power, he made humanity as male and female so they could share with him the love he felt for all his creation and the reproductive capacity to perpetuate the human species.

And so it was that on Thursday, February 19, 1914, Charles William Kram and Emma Zander presented themselves before the Rev. Francis Machan, the Catholic priest at Sts. Cyril and Methodius Church in Shiner, Texas, for the Holy Sacrament of Matrimony.

After the customary exchange of vows and the declaration of intentions, the couple received the blessings of God upon their union.

It was a glorious day for the Kram and Zander families, but especially for Charles and Emma.

According to a news report in the March 3, 1977, edition of *The Shiner Gazette*, Mr. Kram had been born June 4, 1887, in Eichenzell, Hessen, Nassau, Kasil Province, Germany. This son of Pius and Karolina Auth Kram came to America with his family in 1894, a mere seven-year-old boy. He grew up in the Shiner area where he became well known and highly regarded as a successful farmer.

Miss Zander, on the other hand, was a native of Shiner who was born of German immigrants. Her father, Wilhelm (William) Zander, came to America in 1876 and her mother, Marie Katlke Zander, arrived in 1877. They met and married in 1878. Emma Zander had been born December 9, 1892, the youngest of seven children.

Life in the new world was filled with opportunities to make the best of one's present circumstances. Father Charles Kram, Jr., once related in one of his homilies that his mother often told him how, in her childhood, she made a doll by putting clothes she had made on a corncob.

Make the best you can of your present circumstances. That seemed to be the guiding principle for the Kram family. We will see evidence of this truth throughout the story of this remarkable family.

Charles and Emma settled on a sixty-nine-acre farm two miles east of Shiner in Lavaca County and began their life together, a life that spanned sixty-three years. The years were filled with hard work, enormous love of God and family and neighbor, good food, and gratitude for all the gifts from God and the opportunities this land offered them.

1914 was a difficult time for a young family to be formed. Economic pressures created an atmosphere of frugality and skillful management of time and money. Citizens of German heritage felt social pressures from the political unrest in Europe that involved Germany and its neighbors. Fortunately, the population in and around Shiner contained sufficient numbers of German families to provide reasonable comfort. And there was always the Church, where love of God and neighbor transcended all else.

Charles was a devout Catholic and faithfully practiced his religion. Emma had been raised in the Lutheran faith, but since she married a Catholic, she attended church with her husband. In time, she formally joined the Catholic Church. She was instrumental in raising the children in the Catholic faith.

We begin to see a pattern developing: *Make the best you can of your present circumstances.*

It was not long before the family began to grow. On August 18, 1915, a son was born. He was named Edgar Pius (for his grandfather Pius Kram) and Wilhelm (for his grandfather Wilhelm Zander). This brought much joy to the young Kram family. Edgar and his future siblings were born in the Wagner Hospital, cared for by Dr. Frank Wagner, one of the most outstanding physicians in Texas. On October 21, 1921, the family was saddened when Isabella Gertrude died at birth. In time, great joy was evident when another daughter named Felicia was born on December 6, 1927. Finally, on September 30, 1929, another son, Charles William Kram, Jr., was born.

This story is about the youngest child, who grew up to be the remarkable Fr. Charles, the quadriplegic priest who served for nearly twenty-five years as a hospital chaplain doing what he enjoyed most in life: serving God and neighbor with an enormous amount of love.

During his hospital chaplaincy, in a homily on the parable in which Jesus compared the kingdom of heaven to leavened bread, Fr. Charles told how his mother used yeast to make bread at home. He said the yeast was a little piece of dough saved from a previous baking, which had fermented, and which was mixed with the new dough. His mother, he said, used to call it everlasting yeast because it went from one batch of bread to another. She would keep it in a pint jar with a glass lid. The yeast would rise and tilt the lid and she would say, "It's tipping its hat."

He went on to speak of the transforming power of yeast. "It changed the character of the bread. Unleavened bread is hard and dry and unappetizing, but bread baked with yeast is soft and spongy and tasty," he said.

He concluded by saying that just as leaven transforms bread dough, so, too, the coming of Christ's kingdom transforms human life.

That's exactly what Christian love does in a family, and the Kram family was built on Christian love.

The family attended church at Sts. Cyril and Methodius Catholic Church in Shiner, Texas. Shiner was in the Archdiocese of San Antonio at the time and was served by archdiocesan priests.

Charles received his first sacrament, baptism, on October 15, 1929. Father L. P. Netardus was the presiding clergyman. His sponsors were his uncle and aunt, William and Helen Kram. And so, young Charles's Christian life was put into motion.

The Pre-High School Years

In one of Fr. Charles's homilies, he made this observation: "Ordinarily, the notions of right and wrong that we live by all our lives are determined in early childhood. 'As the twig is bent, the tree's so inclined.' Just as a sapling must be braced up and protected if it is to grow up straight, so, too, without guidance and correction, even the best kind of person can go astray."

In another homily, he remarked; "Early formation is so important. Let me give you an example from my childhood. There was an old tree in our pasture that had grown so bent over that I could almost walk up the side of the trunk. It was a fine example of the old saying, 'As the twig is bent, the tree's so inclined.' A child will usually be, all his life, like the parents trained him in his early years."

The Kram children grew up in a loving, secure, responsible atmosphere guided by parents devoted to each other and to the family.

Edgar was fourteen years older than Charles, but Charles and his sister, Felicia, were a little less than two years apart.

Felicia recalls that she and Charles played marbles under the shade of the big trees in the yard. They also played "hide and seek" and other children's games when there was time.

A childhood friend and cousin recalls that after church on Sundays, the families would gather at each other's house to visit and share a meal. The children played the games of that time, such as "kick the can," "flying dutchman," "hide and seek," "in and out the window," and "drop the handkerchief."

The children liked going to a great aunt's house because she lived near a school and they could play on the playground equipment.

Another favorite place for all the children was the Kram residence because it had an attic where they could play make believe with all the things stored up there.

The parents assigned various responsibilities to the children according to their ages and capabilities. For example, when Edgar was younger, he fed the chickens, turkeys, and guinea hens and gathered the eggs. As he got older, he advanced to caring for the hogs and cattle, while Charles assumed the duties with the poultry. Felicia helped her mother with the household work and the cooking and baking. In this way she learned the homemaking lessons she would need later in life when she married and became a mother.

Family chores were an important part of growing up. They were a way of learning the value of accepting responsibility for things that needed to be done and of seeing the rewards of a job well done. These lessons sprang from the love of God and one another the parents instilled in their children.

The education of the children was high on the family's list of priorities. Naturally, their education began at home, where the children learned their prayers, social skills, study habits, and responsibilities to God, family, neighbors, and country.

Bunjes School became the center of their early formal education. The school was located about two miles from their home.

The Texas Historical Commission established a Historical Marker in 2005 titled "Site of Bunjes School," which reads as follows:

On June 25, 1886, H. J. Strunk, a resident of Colorado County, Texas sold five acres of land for use as a school and cemetery to the Shinerville School Community. Originally named for area landowner H. B. Shiner. Residents funded, built and staffed the new schoolhouse, shipping lumber in from Flatonia (20 miles NW) and assisting in carpentry work. They soon renamed it Shiner School No. 2 to avoid confusion with the city school in nearby Shiner. A later name change honored trustee Ferdinand Bunjes, who had led a bucket brigade that saved the building when the roof caught fire.

The school initially offered classes up to grade six but added more grades over the years. Patrons built a teacherage for William Fertsch and his wife, and in 1895 the community added an acre of land, as well as a road that helped students access the school.

In early years, attendance was irregular. In 1916, the State of Texas mandated a six-month school year, but absenteeism for agricultural work remained common among farm families. Otto Fisseler taught the school from 1912 to 1919 when he was replaced by Charles Chovanetz, who taught with his wife, Martha, until 1951. During their tenure, in 1933, a fire destroyed the teacherage. The district recovered from the loss and also constructed a new schoolhouse in 1937.

The Great Depression, World War II, and educational reform eventually resulted in the consolidation of such rural school districts in Texas, and in 1951, Bunjes School District No. 20 merged with Shiner Independent School District. The schoolhouse later became a residence, but the history of Bunjes School remains a reflection of the community's early educational efforts.

Charles attended Bunjes School for grades one through four and seven through ten.

In an effort to heighten his religious education, his parents sent him to St. Ludmila's Academy in Shiner for grades five, six, eleven, and twelve.

During his time at Bunjes School, Charles was taught all the subjects by Charles and Martha Chovanetz, a very remarkable pair of educators.

We will learn later in the story of Charles Kram's life that he was conversant in German and Spanish as well as in English. There is no doubt he gained much of this ability from Martha Chovanetz.

He was also skilled in Latin, but credit for exposure to that language must be given to the staff at St. John's Seminary later in his life.

Mrs. Chovanetz had considerable praise for Charles's mental alertness and friendly disposition. She once related to his mother a funny story from his time in the first grade. The students always started the day by singing patriotic and religious songs to set the tone for their day of studying. One morning when she asked the students which song they wanted to start with, Charles quickly raised his hand and suggested, "Miss Martha, can we sing 'Isle of Capri'?" She was surprised and amazed that such a young boy would be attached to a song that was a popular hit of the time, and especially a song with such a romantic theme.

His sister Felicia recalls that he was a gentle person. He didn't get into fights or arguments. He got along well with other children and enjoyed playing games. He liked to help others and to share his belongings with the other children.

A cousin remembers Charles as being a very smart and sweet boy, but one who also loved to joke and play tricks on others. She said he loved to do magic card tricks and play the game of "guess which cup a pea was hidden under." He was also skilled at carving small animals from wood.

He was active in the 4-H Club popular at the time. He loved working with, caring for, and being around farm animals.

His cousin Elton Zander and Zander's wife Lillie tell how handy Charles was with his hands. They say he made a hand-carved sailboat that was exceptionally good for his age, especially without use of special tools. Somehow, he knew he had to soak the wood in water to make the curves in the wood, and the whole project turned out beautifully.

Charles gave the boat to Elton who, years later, donated it to the auction at the Sts. Cyril and Methodius Church festival, where it sold at a good price.

His friends still rejoice in recalling his sense of humor. When the students were having an exposition, Charles entertained them with his production of "The Greatest Swimming Match" and "Walking on Water." "The Greatest Swimming Match" featured a burned match floating in a pan of water. "Walking on Water" took more ingenuity. For that, Charles poured some water on the ground and then walked on it.

Such a lively sense of humor and inventiveness were evidenced throughout his life.

He often boasted that when he graduated from the tenth grade at Bunjes School, he ranked first in a class of two.

Many years later in one of his homilies on the seriousness of an offense being dependent on the circumstances, he told this story:

Back in the 1940s, when I was in Boy Scout Troop 232, we used to go camping every once in a while. On one such camp-out a fellow Scout threw an egg at my little tent and left a yellow smear. This annoyed me greatly because my mother had personally made the tent for me. To make it worse, a mouse later gnawed at the smear and ate a hole into the tent. What if the same Scout had thrown an egg at the President of the United States instead of me? That would have been much worse. The reason is that the seriousness of an offense is measured by the dignity of the one offended. I was just a fellow Scout, the President is the head of a nation.

The High School Years

In Texas, high school consisted of grades nine through twelve. For reasons of economics, Charles's parents had him complete grades nine and ten in Bunjes School, which was the local public school.

They did permit him to go to St. Ludmila's Academy in Shiner for grades eleven and twelve. St. Ludmila's Academy (SLA) was the Catholic school associated with Sts. Cyril and Methodius Church where the family worshiped. Charles had attended SLA for grades five and six and he knew all his classmates.

He was well liked by the students and teachers and he was considered a good student.

The school annual for his junior year contained these comments about Charles: "CHARLES KRAM, the future head of the Department of Agriculture, is quiet, dignified, and has a very charming manner about him. He is president of the boys 4-H Club. Charles is sporting a badge on his sweater that loudly proclaims him a member of the National Vegetable Growers Association."

There were seven boys and seven girls in his junior class and they were a lively group that the school proclaimed to be worth knowing.

As a teenager, Charles enjoyed going to community dances. He was a good dancer and was popular with the girls. One of his teenage friends recalls that she wasn't often asked to dance by the other boys, but Charles often asked her to join him on the dance floor. She said he always made her feel special and not simply a wallflower. She remembers him as kind and considerate, but not necessarily "holy." He was just a fine young man. She was Lutheran and he was Catholic, and she was surprised when he entered the seminary.

A cousin also recalls that as a teenager, Charles was a good dancer and popular with the girls, who were thrilled when he asked them to dance, as he was tall and handsome. She recalls that he was the best-looking boy in the family.

In his teens, he was interested in many things. It was a time of becoming who he was to be, of finding his own identity. Sometimes, this was a real challenge. He was well liked by his peers, boys and girls alike. Should that lead to public service of some sort? He was a good student, inquisitive by nature, always asking questions and exploring new things. Should he become an educator? He was comfortable with languages; German and Spanish were as easy to use as was his native English. Where should that take him? He liked animals and was good working with them. Should he follow the path of his father in the world of agriculture? He loved jokes and entertaining people. Is the entertainment field meant to be his calling?

What is a young man to do?

In the spiritual atmosphere of the Catholic school, he experienced the power of prayer. From time to time he went to church to pray. He found great comfort and consolation from visits to the Blessed Sacrament, when he felt alone with God. Sometimes during these prayerful moments, he felt God was calling him to serve the Church as a priest. But, no—that seemed too lofty. He didn't deem himself worthy of such a vocation.

He had never even served as an altar boy at Mass, and he wasn't drawn to the Church through admiration for any particular priestly model. Yet the attraction to the priesthood was strong at times. It would come and go, much like the pendulum of a clock. No matter where his thoughts wandered, they always returned to God.

He was sure that every true vocation is an invitation from God, and whether one follows that calling closely depends to a great extent on the advice and example of other people.

He had no priestly model whom he admired, but there was a nun in his life who spoke glowingly of spiritual perfection and the value of managing your time well and for beneficial purposes. She guided the young people toward the goal of strengthening their wills and their characters by making small sacrifices and being alert for opportunities of grace.

This nun was Sr. Anthony, and she spoke with love and authority in a convincing manner. Charles related later in life that she talked to them about the shortness of their lives. She told them they should waste none of their precious lives, but to do everything in service of God. Her advice fell in line with the family discipline of making the best of your situation no matter what the circumstances.

Her enthusiastic love of God sparked Charles to open his heart and mind to God's call to "come, follow me." He felt the same urge to accept God's call as Simon and Andrew felt when Jesus told them to come after him and he would make them fishers of men. It was God's call to him to be a priest. He felt sure of that.

His reasons for wanting to be a priest centered on his realization that the time for preparation for eternity was short in relation to the endlessness of eternal life. Sister Anthony was right; laying treasures in heaven was more secure than treasures on earth. Time is short but the rewards are great. Priestly life was the means to this end.

With that decision made, soon after his high school graduation Charles informed Fr. Netardus, his pastor, of his desire to be a priest. Father Louis Netardus had been pastor in Shiner for many years and he knew the Kram family well. He was moved with urgency because the next class in the seminary was already formed. Father Netardus discussed Charles's decision with his parents and found them supportive of his decision. He then discussed the matter with the admissions staff at St. John's Seminary in San Antonio, who pressed him for details of Charles's qualifications. Impressed with the enthusiastic endorsement of Charles's pastor, the seminary officials led by Fr. James Stakelum accepted the young man as a student subject to the approval of the archbishop of San Antonio.

Father Netardus presented his case to Archbishop Robert E. Lucey. The archbishop considered carefully all the reasons for accepting the young man. Moved by Fr. Netardus's strong support plus the fact that church records showed that Sts. Cyril and Methodius Church had already produced six priests from its families, the archbishop approved Charles Kram's admission into the seminary.

God has ways of getting things done, and Charles's future was suddenly in overdrive.

CHAPTER TWO

St. John's Seminary

The Word of the Lord came to me thus: "Before I formed you in the womb, I knew you, before you were born, I dedicated you, a prophet to the nations I appointed you."

"Ah, Lord God!" I said, "I know not how to speak, I am too young."

But the Lord answered me, "Say not I am too young. To whomever I send you, you shall go; whatever I command you, you shall speak.

Have no fear before them, because I am with you to deliver you," says the Lord. (Jeremiah 1:4–8)

Charles was very much aware of the presence of God in his life, and he understood that each of us somehow fits into God's plan for the world, and the role we fill is our vocation or "calling."

He lived by the teaching of Cdl. John Henry Newman, the saintly English church leader who lived from 1801 to 1890. His teaching on vocation was this:

> God created me to do him some definite service. He has committed some work to me that he has not committed to another. I have my mission; I never may know it in this life; but I shall be told it in the next.

> I have a part in a great work; I am a link in a chain, a bond of connection between persons. He has not created me for naught.

I shall do good. I shall do his work; I shall be an angel of peace, a preacher of truth in my own place, while not intending it, if I do but keep his commandments in my calling.

With this commitment in mind, Charles entered St. John's Seminary.

St. John's Seminary in San Antonio, Texas, was established by the Most Reverend John Shaw, bishop of the Diocese of San Antonio, on October 2, 1915.

In 1926, the diocese was elevated to the status of archdiocese. Following the death of Archbishop Arthur J. Drossaerts on September 8, 1940, Bishop Robert E. Lucey of the Amarillo diocese was named archbishop.

The seminary was located adjacent to Mission Concepcion, more properly named Mission Señora de la Purisima Concepcion de Acuna on Mission Road. A new three-story building had been built to house this important educational institution. It was staffed by priests of the Vincentian Fathers of the Congregation of the Missions.

The domestic staff of Josephine Sisters provided the food and housekeeping needs of the students and staff who lived in the seminary facilities.

Charles William Kram, Jr., arrived at the seminary in September 1946, less than thirty days before his seventeenth birthday. In his words, "the first few days were hectic." This was nothing like life on the farm near Shiner. Gone were his parents and older brother and sister. Here were boys and young men of all ages in regimented living conditions. Everything was done on a timed schedule. The clock determined when you got up, when you got cleaned up and dressed, when you ate, when you went to class, when you studied, and when you went to bed. And, always, there were times for prayer. There was little time to be homesick. You still loved your family, but there was no time to dwell on them. Life was structured and committed to change. The life of a person committed to serving God was different from that of a person committed to temporal affairs.

The schedule of classroom work was heavy. At the level at which Charles entered the seminary, he was taking freshman college courses. In addition, he had some catching up to do, as those students who entered the seminary for their high school studies had already been introduced to advanced religious courses beyond what he had received at St. Ludmila's Academy, even though it was a Catholic high school. Seminary studies were just so much more intense. There was much to learn. He felt fortunate, though, as the professors were all trained specifically for this environment, and they were able to help him make the transition. He felt fortunate for having an excellent spiritual director who guided him through this formative process. How can you feel like you know so little when you have already learned so much? And yet there was so much more to learn.

Seminary life was challenging and certainly not boring. Classroom work and studies were fast-paced. One of his professors observed that Charles was such a gentle person he wondered if the young man would be able to handle the demands of the formative process. Yet this same teacher admired his fortitude and perseverance.

Fortunately, Charles had an inquiring mind, and he absorbed and digested information easily. Church teachings, Church history, Scripture, Latin, and Worship Rituals challenged even good students, but Charles had learned to handle burdens early in life. His parents, as well as his early educators, were excellent teachers who expected excellence in all matters and gave the opportunities to achieve one's mental capacities.

We must never forget the role that prayer played in Charles's formation and later life. It was a normal part of everyday living in the seminary.

Charles recalled once that, as a boy, he sometimes wondered whether it was permissible to say his night prayers in bed or must he always be kneeling or standing. He chuckled when he said one of his professors, a priest, said he sometimes said his official prayers while soaking in the bathtub. Praying, after all, is simply the lifting up of one's mind to God, and the most important part of praying is quietly listening to God.

The family theme he learned at home served Charles well as he faced all the challenges of growing in knowledge and wisdom and reverence for God as well as growing in physical and mental maturity.

Make the best you can of your present circumstances.

It was early in life that Charles learned the lesson that if God gives you a job to do, surely he will give you the tools with which to do it. The secret in life was to properly use the tools God has given you.

Ever present in the mind of this young man were the life, examples, and teachings of his father and mother, Charles and Martha Chovanetz at Bunjes School, Sister Anthony at SLA, and Fr. Louis Netardus at Sts. Cyril and Methodius Church in particular, as well as the other fine dedicated people whose lives touched him.

There is no way to forget that his home church had already produced six priests to serve God. Among them were:

Fr. Francis Havel, ordained July 15, 1916

Fr. Louis Blinka on March 25, 1930

Fr. Edward Jansky on March 25, 1930

Bishop John Morkovsky on December 15, 1933

Fr. Julius Petru on April 15, 1937

Fr. Albert Manath on April 15, 1937

Church records show that seven more men from this church became priests:

Fr. Emil Wesselsky, ordained March 17, 1956

Fr. Lawrence Matula on May 26, 1962

Fr. Joseph Hybner on May 26, 1963

Fr. Timothy Kosler on April 25, 1971

Fr. Charles Kram, Jr., on December 5, 1975

Fr. David Berger on June 3, 2006

Fr. Gabriel Espinosa on June 16, 2007

This is truly a remarkable contribution to the Church by the people of Sts. Cyril and Methodius Church in Shiner.

In telling his own story, Charles expressed his great joy when he was accepted to advance to the first step toward the priesthood, ordination into the Order of Subdeacon. It was at this point that final preparations were made for his priestly ordination. He would commit himself to a life of chastity and celibacy and to total consecration to serving God and his Church.

One more year of intense study and formation for the priesthood remained, and the fruits of his preparation would be realized. He once recalled how inadequate he felt as he approached ordination as a subdeacon. His prayer life had always been important to him, and he intensified his call to God for support. He made a seven-day retreat of intense prayer and reflection, and he was strengthened beyond his expectations. He was nearly overcome with joy when he was accepted for ordination.

And so it was that on Friday, May 30, 1952, in San Fernando Cathedral in San Antonio, Texas, the Most Reverend Robert E. Lucey presided over the ordination of five men, three of whom (Thomas A. Lyssy, Lambert P. Laskowski, and Robert J. Walden) were ordained to the Sacred Order of Priesthood and two (Charles W. Kram, Jr., and William F. Halata) to the Sacred Order of Subdeacon.

Following the ceremony in the cathedral and the joyous celebration, the new clergymen went their separate ways. The new priests went to their assignments of service and the subdeacons to their summer ministry, all after a brief vacation at home.

Normally, summer breaks from school were spent teaching Catechism in some parish after a short break at home. This year Charles was to join several other seminarians in "street preaching" in San Antonio. It was a time to be "among the people" and to develop some preaching and teaching techniques.

This was an experience he joyfully anticipated.

Reverend Mr. Kram and Rev. Mr. Halata were to return to the seminary in September for their final year of Theology, known as Theology IV.

It is interesting to note the names of the seminarians for the Archdiocese of San Antonio who were to return for their studies in September 1952.

They were:

THEOLOGY IV:

William Halata and Charles Kram, Jr.

THEOLOGY III:

Benjamin Bonazza, James Brunner, Henry Hilscher, and George Stuebben

THEOLOGY II:

Michael Canney, Gilbert Cruz, Raymond Garcia, Randolph Gronle, Charles Herzig, William Nypaver, Sherill Smith, Lawrence Stuebben

THEOLOGY I:

Louis Fritz, Charles Grahmann, Alton Rudolph, Emil Wesselsky, and John Yanta

PHILOSOPHY II:

James Brandes and Henry Casso

PHILOSOPHY I:

John Bily, Aloysius Leopold, and John Triggs

These men are all well known throughout South Texas for their service to the Church. These two distinguished themselves as bishops:

The Most Reverend Charles Grahmann was bishop of the Diocese of Victoria in Texas and later was bishop of the Diocese of Dallas.

The Most Reverend John Yanta was Auxiliary bishop of the Archdiocese of San Antonio and later was bishop of the Diocese of Amarillo.

Before his ordination as bishop of the Diocese of Victoria in Texas, Msgr. Charles Grahmann was instrumental in expediting Charles Kram's ordination to the priesthood, as we will see later in this story.

CHAPTER THREE

In the Throes of Adversity

In the land of Uz there was a blameless and upright man named Job, who feared God and avoided evil. Seven sons and three daughters were born to him; and he had seven thousand sheep, three thousand camels, five hundred yoke of oxen, five hundred she-asses, and a great number of work animals, so that he was greater than any of the men of the East. (Job 1:1–3)

And so one day, while his sons and daughters were eating and drinking wine in the house of their eldest brother, a messenger came to Job and said, "The oxen were plowing and the asses were grazing beside them, and the Sabeans carried them off in a raid. They put the herdsmen to the sword, and I alone have escaped to tell you." While he was yet speaking, another came and said, "Lightning has fallen from heaven and struck the sheep and their shepherds and consumed them; and I alone have escaped to tell you." While he was yet speaking, another came and said, "The Chaldeans formed three columns, seized the camels, carried them off and put those tending them to the sword, and I alone have escaped to tell you." While he was yet speaking, another came and said, "Your sons and daughters were eating and drinking wine in the home of their eldest brother, when suddenly a great wind came across the desert and smote the four corners of the house. It fell upon the young people and they are dead, and I alone have escaped to tell you." He cast himself prostrate upon the ground and said, "Naked I came forth from my mother's womb, and naked shall I go back again. The Lord gave and the Lord has taken away; blessed be the name of the Lord!"

In all this Job did not sin, nor did he say anything disrespectful of God. (Job 1:13–22)

We reflect here on the adversity of Job's life for a glimpse of how suddenly the course of one's life can change. We are about to witness the collapse of Charles's world as he had expected it to unfold.

He was at home with his parents for a short summer vacation before embarking on a summer of street preaching in San Antonio and the neighboring towns when he became ill.

He later recalled that it all began on Wednesday, June 11, 1952. He felt like he was coming down with the flu, and he had a pain between his shoulders. The doctor examined him and had him admitted into the hospital. He was treated for his symptoms, but early Sunday morning paralysis set in. Fortunately, Dr. Frank Wagner was there. He immediately recognized the symptoms as the onset of polio. The disease was so quick to act and so deadly that there was no time to lose. The local hospital was not equipped to deal with this killer; iron lungs were the life-savers and they were expensive. Arrangements were made to transport him immediately to Robert B. Green Hospital in San Antonio, a two-hour trip.

It was believed that he probably wouldn't survive the trip. The local priest was called and Father (later Monsignor) Stanley Petru rushed to the scene and administered the sacrament of extreme unction, now called the sacrament of anointing the sick. Monsignor Petru recalls that Charles was very ill, semi-conscious, and struggling to stay alive. The good priest had already ministered to several polio victims who did not survive and he was sure Charles would also not make it through the night. He prayed as fast and as sincerely as he could. He anointed the young man before they moved him to the ambulance. Charles was now in the hands of God.

It was Sunday, June 15, 1952, a day the Kram family never forgot.

Polio (Paralytic Poliomyelitis), sometimes called Infantile Paralysis, is a viral infectious disease in which the spinal cord becomes inflamed and nerves are damaged or destroyed. In the 1950s, before an effective vaccine was developed, the disease created a reign of terror among the people as it struck mainly young people, many of them mere children. Those who did not die were left paralyzed or deformed. Two types of paralysis occurred depending on the nerves that were involved: Spinal Polio, the most common form, affected the legs, while Bulbar Polio resulted in damage to the muscles utilizing cranial nerves, nerves that originated in the brain. The brain was not affected—only the nerves emerging from there.

Charles was stricken with a combination of these two varieties, commonly called Bulbospinal Polio. It was particularly devastating as it left him paralyzed from the neck down. This cruel disease had its "good-news, bad-news" characteristics. The good news was that it did not alter or affect his mental capabilities, his feeling of pain or pleasure, or his bodily functions, internal organs, or any of his senses. The bad news was he could not operate his legs or feet, he had limited use of his hands, arms, and shoulders, and he could not operate the muscles of his chest—hence, he could not breathe on his own.

This devastating condition left him virtually helpless. He was totally dependent on help from others for all physical activities.

Help in breathing was the most critical and immediate need. We are all aware that breathing is essential to survival. The body needs a constant exchange of gases; oxygen must be brought into the body and carbon dioxide must be removed. This process is accomplished by our breathing activity. To make this activity more urgent, the process must be immediate and continuous. We have no capacity for storing oxygen in the body for later use or for emergencies.

Every cell of the body is dependent on an adequate supply of oxygen and the removal of the corresponding waste product, carbon dioxide. Inadequate or suspended breathing hampers the functioning of each cell in the body. As cells malfunction from lack of oxygen, they begin to starve to death, and each appropriate organ begins to stop functioning, resulting in the person's death.

Since proper breathing is dependent on the operation of the chest muscles and diaphragm, it is easy to see how important these organs are to life.

To facilitate the breathing process in polio patients, breathing assistance was the first order of treatment. A device called an iron lung assisted the patient in the breathing process.

An iron lung is a mechanical breathing apparatus consisting of an airtight metal cylinder into which the patient's entire body, except the head, is enclosed. By alternately decreasing and increasing the air pressure in the tank-like device, the patient is forced to inhale oxygen and exhale carbon dioxide, both processes that are essential to life.

The proper name for the iron lung is negative pressure ventilator. This life-saving device was invented in 1927 by Harvard medical researchers Philip Drinker and Louis Agassiz Shaw.

The nearest and most suitable hospital for polio patients was the Robert B. Green Hospital, where the patient could be placed in an iron lung. The trip to San Antonio was critical. Speed was essential, but so was safety. The most critical aspect, though, was to keep Charles breathing during the whole trip. Medics in the ambulance alternated administering artificial respiration through compression of his chest. For the two-hour trip, you can easily see how tiring this is for the medical personnel. But they have committed their lives to preserving life and they are truly our heroes.

This group of unsung heroes safely delivered Charles to the hospital. The personnel there had been alerted to his pending arrival. Upon his arrival at the hospital, he was immediately placed in an iron lung.

Charles's condition had worsened during the trip from Shiner, and he spent the next three weeks in a delirious condition, sometimes conscious and sometimes unconscious. His survival remained uncertain. Paralysis was complete. Considerable joy and hope prevailed when he was able to wiggle one toe. Charles later recalled that fellow patients had died on his right and his left, even with the marvelous help of the iron lung. For some unknown reason, his life had been spared.

He never lost his faith in God. That faith is what sustained him through his whole ordeal. Without it, there would be little to hold on to in this terrible situation. He would later see that God had plans for him, but for now, there was only his faith in God. He found solace in the teachings of the Church and the Scripture readings he had studied. For example, Matthew 11:28–30 tells us that God will give us the strength to carry any burden when we are living our lives according to his will. How comforting that is! Also, "We know that all things work for good for those who love God, who are called according to his purpose" (Romans 8:28) and "I consider that the sufferings of this present time are as nothing compared with the glory to be revealed to us" (Romans 8:18) and "Do not ignore this one fact, beloved, that with the Lord one day is like a thousand years and a thousand years are like one day" (2 Peter 3:8).

Charles sustained his hope and faith with his love of God. In his writings, he displayed those attributes. An example is this, from his writings: "We see God's Will not only in his commands and counsels but also in his good pleasure in all the events to which his plan would have us submit for our own advancement in holiness and for his everlasting glory."

In an interview with Mary Butschek on March 9, 2005, Msgr. Stanley Petru expressed these thoughts about the future Fr. Charles Kram:

He was a saint before he died. Really. That Sunday in 1952 when I anointed him in Shiner, he was very ill. He was sort of semi-conscious and I didn't think he would live. I thought he would die. And then I went to see him in the iron lung in San Antonio. SUCH PATIENCE! And I realized that it was God's Will, that he was picked by the Lord to go through this, just like he was picked by the Lord to teach all of us priests a lesson to be obedient regardless of what happens to us, we have to take it and carry our cross willingly and put up with it. He was a perfect example of patience and resignation to the Will of Almighty God. That's why when I read the lives of the saints, I often wonder, you know, if he had some special spiritual experiences. He must have had, because it doesn't seem like he was ever discouraged or lacking energy to do what he was asked to do.

Those are endearing thoughts from a man who himself is a holy and loving servant of God.

At this point in life, Charles Kram was truly at a change in the direction of his life. He suddenly went from seminarian ordained as subdeacon who would soon be ordained a priest, to a helpless invalid who literally depended entirely on other people for his existence—and yet, his faith in God was unchanged.

Here are some thoughts from his writings:

Our state of life gives an indication of what God expects of us. But these things can suddenly change. Life can take unexpected turns. One door may close so that another door can open. Sometimes the only thing we have to hang on to is the thought that God makes all things work together for our final happiness and for his everlasting glory. One saintly person was asked what he would do if God were suddenly to tell him that he was about to die. His reply was that he would continue doing what he was doing. Indeed, what could be more perfect or more acceptable than always to do what God expects of us? That is also what Jesus meant when he prayed those agonizing prayers in the garden, "May Thy Will be done." Because of his patient endurance of the cross, Jesus accomplished his Father's Will, rose gloriously from the dead, ascended to his Father's right hand, and prepared a place for us. So, too, as we each continue to struggle with life's problems, and continue to fulfill all that God has called us to do, we keep our eyes on the future, a hundred years from now, a million years from now, when we will know in every detail, what God's purpose was for each of us.

And so, Charles accepted his suffering patiently with full knowledge that the best part of life was still ahead of him.

Charles later recalled this part of his life and wrote these thoughts:

Following the Will of God wherever it may lead should be the ideal of every Christian. Although I could not know God's purpose in choosing me, I felt that his present will for me was to be a good patient. I tried to be cheerful and cooperative and tried to get well.

We are reminded here of this teaching from the Gospel according to John 11:1–4:

Now a man was ill, Lazarus from Bethany, the village of Mary and her sister Martha. Mary was the one who had anointed the Lord with perfumed oil and dried his feet with her hair; it was her brother Lazarus who was ill. So the sisters sent word to him (Jesus), saying, "Master, the one you love is ill." When Jesus heard this, he said, "This illness is not to end in death, but is for the glory of God, that the Son of God may be glorified through it."

We continue with Charles's recollections of his recovery: "In February 1953, I was transferred [from Robert B. Green Hospital in San Antonio] to Gonzales Warm Springs for rehabilitation."

Gonzales Warm Springs, located near the town of Gonzales, was the leading rehabilitation facility in Texas for the care of polio victims during the polio epidemic of the 1940s and 1950s. It was built around an artesian well that flowed with hot mineral waters. Its revolutionary treatment developed by Sr. Elizabeth Kenny of the University of Minnesota utilized hot pads and pool therapy to aid in promoting muscle rehabilitation. Its heroic success in polio treatment is well documented.

Charles's writings on his recovery time at the Warm Springs facility includes these comments:

Physical Therapy, Occupational Therapy, and a hopeful atmosphere resurrected me out of bed into a wheelchair where my arms were fitted with special braces and slings which enabled me to weave, paint, write, and feed myself. I was also taught to use a rubber-tipped stick held in the teeth for such things as turning pages, typing, and tuning a radio.

In the fall of 1953, he was discharged from Warm Springs. He was sent home to his parents' farm near Shiner. His parents devoted the rest of their lives to caring for him. His physical rehabilitation was as complete as it could be.

He came home with a rocking bed that helped him breathe. He spent the rest of his life depending on that rocking bed to help him. His primary care physician for the last few years, Crayton E. Ciborowski, M.D., described how the rocking bed worked:

> Charles could not breathe at all on his own. All the muscles that move the chest and diaphragm were paralyzed. The iron lung creates a negative pressure that pulls air through the mouth and trachea into the lungs and then creates positive pressure to expel the air. The rocking bed works on the same principle. When the feet are down, the abdominal contents move down with it because of gravity that pulls the diaphragm muscles down and creates a negative pressure in the chest and air enters the lungs. Conversely, when the bed rocks so that the head is down, the abdominal viscera push up on the diaphragm and expels the air from the chest.

This up and down motion is driven by an electric motor and is never-ending as long as the patient is on the bed.

Obviously, this rocking motion requires some "getting used to it" for both the patient and the caregivers. Just imagine trying to do any medical or physical care for a patient that is moving constantly in this manner.

We hear again the attitude of this remarkable family: *Make the best you can of your present circumstances.*

Here at home on the farm with his beloved and devoted mother and father, Charles's journey through life was, indeed, altered. While headed toward the original goal of doing God's will, the direction or course set for him was now changed.

He will never complete his studies at St. John's Seminary. Adversity abounds.

CHAPTER FOUR

The Hand of God

Your hands made me and fashioned me;
give me insight to learn your commands.
Those who fear you rejoice to see me,
because I hope in your word.
I know, Lord, that your edicts are just;
though you afflict me, you are faithful.
May your love comfort me in accord
with your promise to your servant.
Show me compassion that I may live,
for your teaching is my delight.
Shame the proud for oppressing me unjustly,
that I may study your precepts.
Let those who fear you turn to me,
those who acknowledge your decrees.
May I be wholehearted toward your laws,
that I may not be put to shame.
(Psalms 119:73–80)

Charles told this story about his time at home:

Since coming home, time has continued to pass quickly. I keep busy writing and typing, correcting tests for the religious correspondence courses, drawing and painting, watching TV, and operating Ham Radio Station W5TFZ, which by happy coincidence I had set up just a year before the onset of the illness. I also possess a visitor's book, which by now is rich with names of men, women, and children, including the names of two Bishops and one Archbishop. Sometimes people ask whether I would still like to be a priest if I could. The answer is always an emphatic "Yes." In fact, I often dream that I am back at the seminary for that final year.

Charles dreamed of and longed for the priestly ordination that was denied him by his devastating illness, which rendered him unable, according to Church Law, from performing the appropriate functions of celebrating the Mass.

The compilation of Church Law is known as the Code of Canon Law. The version that was promulgated in 1917 was known as the Pro-Benedictine Code of Canon Law, and it remained in effect until it was revised in 1983. Canon 984(3) of the Code in effect at the time of Charles Kram's illness essentially blocked his ordination to the priesthood with the pronouncement that those impaired in body who cannot safely, because of a deformity, conduct ministry of the altar should not be ordained.

Although Charles yearned to be a priest, he yearned more to be a faithful servant of God, no matter how God wanted him to serve. Doing the will of God was paramount in his life. It was evident to him that, somehow, he and his present condition fit into God's plan. He was totally committed to do the will of God, no matter the present cost.

By never complaining about his suffering of pain and the humiliation of his dependency, he raised suffering to the dignity of the divine. In this way, he accepted the circumstances of his life as the will of God. To complain against the will of God would certainly be unworthy of a true Christian. To accept his suffering as the will of God made his suffering a source of joy, a vehicle of unity with God here on earth.

We might ask ourselves how it is that suffering can be a source of joy. We find the answer in 2 Corinthians 1:3–7, where St. Paul teaches us accordingly:

Blessed be the God and Father of our Lord Jesus Christ, the Father of compassion and God of all encouragement, who encourages us in our every affliction, so that we may be able to encourage those who are in any affliction with the encouragement with which we ourselves are encouraged by God. For as Christ's sufferings overflow to us, so through Christ does our encouragement also overflow. If we are afflicted, it is for your encouragement and salvation, if we are encouraged, it is for your encouragement, which enables you to endure the same sufferings that we suffer. Our hope for you is firm, for we know that as you share in the sufferings, you also share in the encouragement.

1 Peter 4:12–13 carries this message one step further:

Beloved, do not be surprised that a trial by fire is occurring among you, as if something strange were happening to you. But rejoice to the extent that you share in the sufferings of Christ, so that when his glory is revealed, you may also rejoice exultantly.

Our young scholar was true to his commitment to serve God, but he recognized how difficult these commitments can be. In later years, when he was ordained a priest, he commented in one of his homilies,

It seems that nowadays it is harder than ever to stand by one's commitment. A friend of mine, because of his commitment to Christ, gave up a high-paying job as a travelling accountant because he was asked to be dishonest. He was willing to make a big change in his life to keep his faith with Christ. Then he found just as good a job in his hometown, where he is secure in life. If you are ever blamed for taking a stand, or for doing things that good Christians are expected to do, consider it a privilege to make the sacrifice. God will provide. There are many callings in life from the cradle to the grave, but the basic and most all-embracing one is the one we made at Baptism when we renounced Satan and turned our lives over to Christ.

Charles was indeed a true scholar, even in his handicapped capacity. His mind was sharp and his memory phenomenal. He was an avid reader and he used talking tapes from the Library of Congress. He had a strong interest in Scripture and studied the Bible as a hungry man approaches a meal. He kept studying theological and philosophical texts and was current on the changes in worship brought about by the Second Vatican Council. He was so well versed in all aspects of the Church that in later years, when his ordination was approved and the archbishop appointed a priest to update Charles on current Church matters, the priest was amazed at how thorough and complete was his self-preparation.

Charles mentioned earlier in this chapter that one of the activities that occupied him during this phase of his life was the operation of Ham Radio Station W5TFZ that he set up a year before the onset of his illness. Charles was introduced to Ham Radio by fellow seminarian Joseph Kolb, who had been in the Army Signal Corp prior to entering St. John's Seminary. Joe had his own radio set-up and was licensed to operate it. He helped Charles learn the procedures of operating an amateur radio station. Through Joe's guidance, Charles secured his license. Charles and Joe were ordained subdeacons together and were to be busy the summer of 1952 with street preaching. Joseph completed his priestly formation and was ordained for the Oklahoma City archdiocese. He and Charles remained close friends the rest of their lives, and Fr. Kolb recalls visiting Charles several times at home and during his hospital ministry. He considered it an honor to be able to attend Charles's ordination in 1975.

During Charles's time in his parents' home, he had his radio equipment set up in his bedroom. From there, he communicated with other radio operators all over the world. His writings confirm that he communicated with operators in over 160 other countries. The Ham Radio experience was so important to him that even when he was in his hospital ministry later and he didn't use the radio, he kept his license current. He even renewed it for ten years in October 1998.

Deacon Linard Harper and his wife, Dot, who knew Fr. Charles after his ordination, related how God had given Charles to such loving and caring parents as Mr. and Mrs. Kram. They had two other children whom they loved very much as well, but somehow they recognized that God had blessed Charles in special ways. Even when he contracted polio and nearly died and then came home as a helpless invalid, they did not lose sight of his special blessings. They felt in their hearts that all that was happening was, somehow, related to the mission in life that God had planned for Charles. From the moment of his illness to their own deaths, they devoted their lives to his care and welfare.

It is easy to become awestruck when you realize that when Charles came home from his rehabilitation at Warm Springs, he was totally dependent on his parents for his very existence. They had to care for him as a twenty-three-year-old man much the way they would have had to care for an infant. Paralyzed from the neck down to his toes, there was little he could do for himself. Yet they never wavered and never complained.

How Charles and his parents managed to continue to maintain their positive attitude is a strong testimony to their trust in and love of God. If one were ever to even consider Charles to be saintly, one must first consider his parents saintly. In caring for their son as they did, they proved themselves to be true servants of God.

His devoted parents cared for him in their home ever since he was discharged from the Warm Springs treatment facility in 1953, except for a short stay in a treatment facility in Colorado.

In his paralyzed condition, he was unable to do much of anything for himself. His mother and father shared the caregiver role, caring for a grown man much as one cares for an infant. Yet everyone who ever visited them testify strongly that they never once heard any of them—mother, father, or son—complain or voice a negative thought about their plight. They accepted life as it was, as the will of God. They possessed a faith in God that was so strong and loyal that all obstacles and hardships were reduced to minor irritants. In fact, Charles often referred to his condition as "this pesky virus."

Charles Kram, Sr., and his wife, Emma Zander Kram, must have been endowed with remarkable genes comparable to their faith in God. Their attention to the needs of their son is an inspiration to us all. They never wavered and they never faltered. But even the finest piece of machinery will eventually begin to wear down. And so it was with Mrs. Kram. Her health began to deteriorate as the ravaging effects of a stroke set in. As time passed, her condition grew more and more pronounced. Mister Kram soon found himself caring for both his wife and his son. Operating the farm with its multiple chores and doing all the household duties in addition to caring for his eighty-one-year-old wife and his son became a bigger challenge than this eighty-seven-year-old man could handle. Something had to change before the old man broke down.

The pressing decision of what to do weighed heavily on Mr. Kram. Always trusting in God, he prayed for guidance. We are not sure exactly what prayers he used, but it is reasonable to believe his thoughts came to Proverbs 3:5–6, which read: "Trust in the Lord with all your heart, on your own intelligence rely not; in all your ways be mindful of him, and he will make straight your path."

After much prayer and soul-searching, the decision was made to send his beloved wife to the loving and professional care of the staff at Trinity Lutheran Home there in Shiner, where he could visit her often. Then, he could direct all his care-giving attention to his son. And so, on April 25, 1974, Emma Zander Kram moved into Trinity Lutheran Home, where she stayed for the rest of her life.

Now, the aged Mr. Kram could concentrate his efforts on caring for his son, Charles.

Other loving and caring persons who encouraged Charles in his new way of life and who were, in turn, encouraged by him, were the students of St. Ludmila's Academy, who visited him often.

We have a wonderful recollection of these visits by Doris Patek, wife of Deacon Paul Patek. Doris was Doris Aschenbeck at the time. She related:

> As a Junior Catholic Daughter in the 1959–1960 era, groups of seventh- and eighth-grade girls attended meetings under the spirited direction of Mrs. F. M. (Marie)

Wagner, who was the local Catholic Daughters of America pioneer for fostering faith at the junior high school level. We had pet projects and Corporal Works of Mercy throughout the year. One of them was to visit the shut-ins of our parish. Our favorite was Charles Kram, who, at the time, was convalescing at home with the help of his parents, after he had contracted a severe case of polio on June 15, 1952. We would sing songs, bring joy and cheer in many ways, while establishing a sense of belonging to the larger church, which included the homebound and the sick. We walked away awestruck and blessed by his exuberance for life, showing us how he used a rubber tipped stick held in his mouth to type, and the sharing of stories as a Ham Radio operator with people all over the world. He had a great sense of humor and he loved people.

Everywhere you turn, everyone you meet in and around Shiner, you find people with similar stories, many stretching from their childhood visits to see him to "cheer him up" on into their adulthood and being helped by him and his positive attitude and loving spirit.

A beautiful remembrance comes from Sr. M. Sylvia Grahmann, IWBS of the Incarnate Word Convent in Victoria, Texas. She knew him from 1971 until 2000. She relates:

Before his ordination to the priesthood, Sister George and I visited with him every Saturday afternoon. We prayed with him, socialized, assisted him with correspondence, and did whatever he wished done. After ordination, we assisted him with offering Mass. He was always in a good mood. He had a fine sense of humor and never complained about how he felt. His gentleness and kindness radiated from him. He was patient, humble, and caring. He was never morose, and looked at the bright side of things. He was interested in what happened in school and in current events. There was no self-pity evident from him.

Sister Sylvia went on:

Since he was a quadriplegic, he was unable to use his hands
(in the normal sense) or his feet (and legs). He spoke with
a halting voice and constantly moved his head while he
spoke. His body jerked as he spoke.

This jerking motion is what enabled him to breathe since he
had no control over his chest muscles and diaphragm, movements
that are essential to breathing.

Sister Sylvia continued:

He was long-suffering, meek, and always even-tempered. I
never witnessed any mood swings. His submission to God's
will was touching. He reminded me of the suffering Christ.
Paralysis, of any nature, is never attractive to me. However,
this did not detract from his saintly qualities. His exuberance and joyfulness overshadowed the effects of his paralysis.

It seemed to Charles and those who knew him that God had
prepared him for this ordeal and for what was to come later in life.
It also appeared that God was preparing him for some future mission.

In his childhood, he occupied himself with what was at hand,
whether it was puttering around in the workshop on the farm,
reading, building model airplanes, making the boat previously
mentioned, doing normal farm chores, or fashioning a child's shoe-
shine kit. Activities such as these plus his devotion to prayer prepared him to handle whatever situation prevailed. He was never
inclined toward self-pity, accepting all circumstances as the will of
God. Even when he became physically impaired by the paralysis,
he never considered himself sick.

Charles's cousin Elton Zander and Zander's wife Lillie relate
that during the summer of 1952, the polio illness struck five young
people in Shiner and several more from other parts of the county.
Some died and some lived. Charles was the most severely affected.
When he returned home after the treatments, his parents took
complete responsibility for his care. They did not hire any help

(until later in life when they were in their 80s). Elton told how every act of care had to be done for him, but his parents willingly and lovingly did everything for him, even little things like combing his hair, brushing his teeth, bathing him, dealing with his bowel and bladder eliminations, and adjusting his sitting and lying down positions to make him comfortable.

The family and neighbors wanted to make life a little more pleasant for him, so they took up a collection to buy a television set, even though none of them had a television in their own homes at the time. During the first few years at home, Charles enjoyed watching TV, but in later years, there were more important things to do. A friend, Victor Novak, set up Charles's Ham radio so he could use a stick in his mouth to dial and work the radio, and that gave him a window to the world. Charles took great joy in being able to talk to many people all over the world. It thrilled him to tell his visitors how many people he reached in so many different places of the world. He also enjoyed drawing and sketching with a pen on a stick held in his mouth. He often drew cartoons or humorous pictures that he gave to family and friends. He learned to type on his electric typewriter that the local Knights of Columbus Council bought for him. When computers became popular, he acquired one and became proficient in its use, again managing the keys with a stick held in his mouth. It's difficult to visualize such skill, but then remember the family theme: *Make the best you can of your present circumstances.*

Elton and Lillie recall that each year for Charles's birthday, Lillie would bake him an angel food cake because she knew that was his favorite dessert. One year when they delivered the cake to the house, no one was at home, so they left it on the kitchen table. Later some other friend baked a devil's food cake, thinking he might like that and left it on the table beside the angel food cake. When the Krams returned home, they laughed, and Charles asked Lillie, "Are ya'll trying to tell me something?" There was always humor to be found in everyday matters.

The Zanders observed that as the years passed, Charles spent his time as best he could. Visitors always came away amazed and edified at the life he lived—a quiet secluded life doing and accepting the will of God.

Lanelle Sommerlatte Kasper was another cousin who recalled fond memories of her and Charles's childhood and later years. They were very near the same age and they lived near each other. They walked to Bunjes School together. She recalled that when she heard Charles was a polio victim, she cried for hours because she realized his whole world would be changed. Even though she was raised in the Lutheran faith, she was very proud that he had gone to the seminary to become a Catholic priest. Now, things are changed, she thought. When she went to visit him, she found he was still the same person as always and was not depressed or angry and had no negative feelings. He was still kind, humorous, happy, intelligent, loving, considerate, and enthusiastic. In his parents' home, he occupied a room next to the dining room on the east side of the house. It was there that he had his Ham radio set up as well as his rocking bed and typewriter.

In a gathering of several nuns who knew Charles both before and after his ordination, Sr. Paschaline Kutac observed that one of his biggest virtues was patience. "I mean," she said, "I always used to say he had the patience of Job. In fact, I think he had more patience than Job had. The simple reason that he could not do a thing for himself and he had to wait for when people had time for him, and he never complained. I don't think I ever heard him complain about anything. He was always grateful for everything that anybody did for him."

Sister Frances Cabrini recalled that one time she took a group of high school juniors to the farm to visit with Charles. She said they went to sing Christmas carols and to bring joy to him. One student was upset about having to go see "this old crippled person." "Why do we have to go see him?" he asked. Sister told him that this is a very saintly person and she thought the youth could get more out of singing Christmas carols for him than anyone might imagine. As it turned out, she remembered that the boy eventually responded favorably and sang enthusiastically after seeing the joy that the occasion brought to Charles. On the bus ride back to town, the boy had a changed attitude and thanked her for including him in the group. She said that Charles had a way about him that brought out the best in whoever visited him.

On December 15, 1969, Charles joined a support group called Catholic Union of the Sick in America, commonly called CUSA. CUSA is an active apostolate which unites disabled or chronically ill members in the Cross of Christ, so that they "find a purpose in suffering." Physical disability or chronic illness is the sole requirement for membership.

Members are united through postal and e-mail group-letters or a cassette group-tape which regularly brings news of the other members of the group, and a message from the group's spiritual advisor. Each member adds a message to the group-letter or tape and sends it to the next group member.

By uniting in CUSA and collectively offering their crosses of suffering to Christ for the benefit of humankind, members help themselves and one another, spiritually and fraternally.

Charles was a member of Tape Group 5. In June 1973, he became leader of his group. Later, following his priestly ordination, he became spiritual advisor of the group. Each group consisted of eight members plus the spiritual advisor.

CUSA was founded on December 8, 1947, by Mrs. Robert Brunner as an American branch of an international Catholic organization of the sick that had been organized thirty-four years earlier in Switzerland, named *L'Union Catholique des Malades*, or UCM. Mrs. Brunner had been a member of that group when she and her husband arrived in the United States in 1939.

Father Charles Kram was the first member of CUSA to be ordained a priest. Father William Wolkovich, who has been spiritual advisor to several tape groups for many years, attended Charles's ordination. He wrote in their monthly newsletter that the most unusual and deeply moving event of his life was sharing in the ordination of the wheelchair-bound CUSAN, Fr. Charles Kram of Shiner, Texas.

But hold it—we're getting ahead of our story.

Reflecting on Charles's active role with this group of fellow sufferers gives us a better understanding into his heroic handling of his own suffering. Members' positive and patient offering of their suffering for the sake of the Kingdom of God is an important lesson we should all learn.

We could all benefit greatly if we prayed daily these beautiful prayers of the CUSA members.

MORNING PRAYER

Dear Lord, here is a new day you have given me in which to love you and help others to love you as well. So that my love for you may be even stronger, help me to spend the hours of this day in your presence, to offer as small sacrifices some of my own little likes and dislikes. Help me not to waste my time in idle pursuits but instead to busy myself to the greatest possible extent in works which are pleasing to you. And above all, help me to love and accept your holy Will.

Lord Jesus, through this cross of my disability, it is your desire to bring me nearer to your divine heart, and especially do you want me to offer my cross, united with your own, in the Holy Sacrifice of the Mass throughout the world, for the salvation of souls.

O my Jesus, help me today not to waste a single one of my trials, both large and small, which, if borne with patience, can obtain so many graces. I desire the Will of the Father, and walking in your footsteps, I accept these trials and offer them to the Father with all my heart in reparation for my sins, for our deceased Cusans, our benefactors—and all those who ask for our prayers, and for the other apostolic intentions which have been entrusted to me.

Bless my brothers and sisters in CUSA, and may we all glorify you and give proof of our love for you by bearing courageously and even joyously the cross which is ours.

Amen.

EVENING PRAYER

O Heavenly Father, another day given me to love you draws to a close. Has it been a day which I can offer lovingly to you? Have my thoughts turned to you frequently this day, and have I tried to be Christ-like in all my contacts with others?

I love you, my God, and I beg forgiveness for any way in which I offended you today.

I cannot undo my petty faults of the day; the unkind retort, my foolish pride, forgetting you for so many hours.

All that remains is a loving regret and a determination to serve you better tomorrow.

Amen.

We have witnessed the love and support in his suffering that Charles received, first from his parents (deep devotion and loving care), then from other family members, the staff at Robert B. Green Hospital and Gonzales Warm Springs Foundation, the clergy and teachers and religious at Sts. Cyril and Methodius Church, students and friends, and finally fellow sufferers in CUSA. There is no room for doubt about the importance of these people in the survival of this victim of a cruel illness with no cure. Taking into account all this love and adding the love of God brings us to understand that something bigger and more important in Charles's life is very near at hand. The force propelling his future ministry was in place and beginning to gain momentum from early in Charles's illness.

As early as February 2, 1954, one of the priests from the area suggested to Archbishop Robert E. Lucey that since he was going to be passing through Shiner on his way to Hallettsville, he might consider stopping at the Kram farm and visit, in his words, "the Reverend Mr. Charles Kram, a subdeacon and a young man who would be a priest of the archdiocese today if the God who writes straight with crooked lines had not let him be stricken with polio a year ago last summer." The archbishop did visit with Charles and his parents and brought great delight to them with his kind thoughtfulness.

The priests of the entire archdiocese kept Charles in their prayers and in their thoughts and spoke frequently to the archbishop about Charles and their desire and hopes that he could be ordained a priest. The archbishop felt kindly toward him and his parents and did his best for them.

On April 5, 1966, Archbishop Lucey wrote a personal letter directly to His Holiness Pope Paul VI requesting permission to ordain Charles to the priesthood. The prayerful approval was not received.

On May 6, 1969, Bishop Francis J. Furey became archbishop. He, too, favored ordaining Charles and petitioned the Vatican for permission to do so, but to no avail. He counseled Charles to develop a ministry in spite of his infirmity to show that he was able to preach and teach the Word of God.

Charles intensified his radio ministry that reached all over the world.

Time went by and the faith of the priest's friends persisted.

The lesson Jesus taught in Matthew 17:20 is well illustrated here. He said, "Amen, I say to you, if you have faith the size of a mustard seed, you will say to this mountain, 'Move from here to there,' and it will move. Nothing will be impossible for you."

And so, the priest's faith was about to move a mountain.

It is amazing how God works. Can you believe how much good can come from a goose hunt? That's right. God used a goose hunt to help those priests move a mountain.

Here is the story as told by the Most Reverend Charles V. Grahmann, Bishop Emeritus of the Diocese of Dallas and first bishop of the Diocese of Victoria in Texas. In his own words:

Charles Kram was a few years ahead of me at St. John's Seminary in San Antonio, Texas. He was from Shiner and I was from Hallettsville, two towns only thirteen miles apart.

Charles was ordained a subdeacon in May 1952. Traditionally a banquet was held for the deacon class before their ordination at the end of May. The subdeacon class was responsible for the program. They had slated Charles to be the Master of Ceremonies. No one expected anything unusual, but he quickly had everyone in a laughing mood. He compared himself to Archbishop Fulton Sheen, the noted TV preacher. I don't remember the many one-liners he used, but I do remember the banquet was one of the funniest events I ever attended.

Shortly after he was ordained a subdeacon, I received word that he had been stricken with polio. An epidemic of polio was present in the area. I was stunned to hear the news and inquired each day of his status. I understood he was rendered totally incapacitated with movement of his neck muscles. I remember his parents pursuing all possible places for treatment. He was in the Robert B. Green County Hospital in San Antonio for a period of time. A faculty member of the seminary brought him the Holy Eucharist each morning. He even was brought one Sunday morning to the seminary for a community Mass. I remember him being rolled in on his hospital rocking bed. It was an awesome moment for all of us seminarians.

After all attempts to find relief, Charles was taken to his family home in Shiner to be cared for by his parents. He was totally incapacitated. One can imagine the burden to care for him placed on his mother and father. But they would have it no other way.

After I was ordained in 1956, on my way to visit my family in Hallettsville, I often stopped in Shiner to visit with Charles. It was only a short distance off Highway 90 on the way from Shiner to Hallettsville. As I recall these visits, he was always happy, with a natural smile on his face. I observed how he was able to learn to do certain things in his incapacitated condition. He would feed himself, write a letter, punch a telephone number or a call button, and operate his Ham radio. I thought how capable humans are to adapt to new, unusual, and restrictive conditions.

In the 1960s a group of priests from San Antonio always journeyed to an annual goose hunt near Garwood, Texas. This took place in January each year. Beginning in 1963, we travelled in two cars to the hunt. We stopped in Shiner to see Charles. Thence, we made this stop a part of our excursion every year.

In 1975, we made our usual stop. When we entered the Kram home, Charles was on his Ham radio. We obviously heard everything he said as well as what the person on the other end was saying. When he finished, he told us that person he was speaking with was in Peru and was a quadriplegic like him. He then shared with us the number of people with Ham radios who were afflicted with similar maladies and would call him for advice, support, and prayers. He had a network of people that called him for spiritual counseling.

When our group departed on that occasion, suddenly Msgr. Alois Goertz remarked: "You know that Charles Kram does more priestly ministry than any of us do. He is daily ministering to all these people all over the world. He ought to be ordained a priest."

That remark didn't fall on deaf ears. Monsignor Tom Lyssy, Father Larry Stuebben, Father John Yanta (later Bishop Yanta), and I (the hunters) all chimed in: "What do we have to do to get him ordained a priest?" The entire time at the hunt was sprinkled with ideas and suggestions. When it was all over, the group instructed me to approach Archbishop Francis Furey and ask that he request Rome for permission to ordain Charles a priest. The norm for ordination precluded one who was physically incapacitated to function.

Returning to my office and work in the Chancery in San Antonio as Archbishop Furey's priest secretary, I wrote him a memorandum making the request. This happened in January 1975. At a meeting to discuss this memorandum, he immediately replied that he would ordain him. I urged him, though, to follow the norm and request permission from the Congregation for Clergy to make an exception and grant permission for the reasons we gave. He said he would do so.

Shortly thereafter, Archbishop Furey went to Rome, stopped by the Congregation and informed them that he was going to ordain as a priest a man who was already ordained a subdeacon but was a quadriplegic. He gave the reason for his request. No one objected, so he assumed an affirmative answer. He called from Rome and instructed me to move ahead with the plans for priestly ordination.

I called Msgr. Stanley Petru, pastor of Sacred Heart Church in Hallettsville and asked him to visit with Charles and inform him of this good news.

Suddenly the magnitude of what was upon us began to sink in. A lot of planning had to go into this miracle of grace. Charles had no updating (as far as we knew) in theology, liturgy, or discipline of the Church since 1952. The Vatican Council had taken place and changes were made. Mass was now in English instead of Latin. I asked Msgr. Stanley Petru of Hallettsville to go once a week and visit with Charles and bring him up to date in the practical aspects in the Church as a result of Vatican II.

While these sessions were taking place, plans were made to move ahead with a date for ordination as a deacon and then to the priesthood. A date was set for Archbishop Furey to go to the home of Charles Kram and ordain him a deacon. That would take place on December 4, 1975. The priestly ordination was set for the next day, December 5, 1975, in Sts. Cyril & Methodius Church in Shiner, Texas.

And so ends Bishop Grahmann's recollection of how this miracle of faith moved the mountain that blocked our hero's ordination to the priesthood.

God truly uses ordinary events, like a goose hunt, to accomplish his goals, doesn't he?

Monsignor Petru had this to say about his assignment to bring Charles up to date before his ordination:

> I was stationed at that time as pastor in Hallettsville and they asked me if I would get Charles ready for ordination, which, of course, was a great privilege. So I helped him. I prepared him for saying Mass, that is, offering the Holy Sacrifice of the Mass. You know someone had to be there always to help him, where his hands were included, in celebrating the Eucharist.

> What surprised me so much was the fact that he was so patient with me and with himself. He never once complained. Then when he was ordained a priest, they had a big celebration. At the banquet after ordination, they asked me to say a few words and I told them, "He remembered everything from the seminary. He was teaching me more than I was teaching him." He didn't have a problem giving spiritual guidance of any sort. It was amazing. He really could read souls.

Suddenly arrangements for the ordination went into motion. They were under the direction of the five priests who were the goose hunters and they left no stone unturned; all stops were released. Invitations were sent to all the clergy and religious of the archdiocese and the seminary and others of Charles's choosing. Also the family and classmates from all his years in school plus the entire parish family were invited. This was to be a liturgical celebration that is seldom, if ever, witnessed in such a rural setting.

All the hoping and waiting and praying and sacrificing would be justified by the celebration that the Church put together.

It is true to say that *the hand of God* was in place.

CHAPTER FIVE

The Anointing

A Reading from the Letter of St. Paul to the Romans:

Just as each of us has one body with many parts, and not all the members have the same function, so too we, though many, are one body in Christ and individually members of another. We have gifts that differ according to the favor bestowed on each of us. One's gift may be prophecy; its use should be in proportion to his faith. It may be the gift of ministry; it should be used for service. One who is a teacher should use his gift for teaching; one with the power of exhortation should exhort. He who gives alms should do so generously; he who rules should exercise his authority with care; he who performs works of mercy should do so cheerfully. (Romans 12:4–8)

This is the Second Reading taken from the Ordination Liturgy celebrated by the Most Reverend Francis J. Furey on December 5, 1975, in Sts. Cyril and Methodius Church in Shiner, Texas, that raised the Reverend Mr. Charles William Kram, Jr., to the Sacred Order of Priesthood.

We might be reminded here that the sacrament of Holy Orders is conferred at three levels or degrees. These are diaconate (deacon), presbyterate (priest), and episcopate (bishop). Only a bishop may administer this sacrament. The sacrament of Holy Orders impresses on the soul of the recipient an indelible mark or character that remains forever; it cannot be erased. Catholic teaching defines this sacrament to be of divine origin.

The order of the Ordination Mass began much like an ordinary Mass except that much fanfare and joyful singing of hymns accompanied the entrance of the ministers of service. After the Liturgy of the Word (the Readings from Scripture and the Homily), the archbishop performed the customary ritual of calling Charles forward to be sure he, the candidate for ordination, was present. He inquired of Charles's teachers if he was worthy of the sacrament. Receiving such assurance, the archbishop asked the people, the gathered congregation, if they approved of the ordination. The church was filled with thunderous applause. Next, the archbishop conducted an examination of the candidate ascertaining his resolve to fully discharge, with the help of the Holy Spirit, the office of priesthood. Everyone then knelt while the archbishop began the prayers for divine blessings upon Charles. The entire congregation then sang the beautiful and prayerful Litany of the Saints. At the conclusion of the Litany of the Saints in which all the saints in heaven were called upon to pray for Charles, the archbishop led the other bishops and all the priests present in silently laying their hands on Charles's head. This is a very moving experience as it involves all the bishops and priests into the consecration of the new priest. It was observed by many of those present that "there was not a dry eye in church" as this ritual unfolded. Archbishop Furey then extended his hands in a prayerful posture and prayed this Prayer of Consecration:

> Come to our aid, O Lord, holy Father, all powerful eternal God, source of every honor and every office. All growth, all permanence comes from you. Yours is the well-ordered plan by which our personalities unfold to ever greater perfection. In keeping with that plan, you instituted sacred rites to fill the ranks of priests and Levites so that you might designate men as next in rank and dignity to the high priests as associates and helpers of those you had appointed to govern your people. So also in the desert you extended the spirit of Moses by infusing that spirit into the minds of seventy wise men, who were his helpers among the people and whom he empowered

to govern that great multitude. You filled the sons of Aaron with their father's power, to make them worthy priests for the offering of saving victims and the celebration of sacred rites. By your Providence, Lord, your Son's apostles had companions of second rank, to help them preach the faith to the whole world. We cannot compare with the high priests, with Moses, Aaron, and the apostles. Weaker than they, so much the more are we in need of help. Grant us that help, O Lord.

We ask you, all-powerful Father, give this servant of yours the dignity of the presbyterate. Renew the Spirit of holiness within him. By your divine gift may he attain the second order in the hierarchy and exemplify right conduct of life.

May he be our fellow-worker, so that the words of the Gospel may reach the farthest parts of the earth, and all nations, gathered together in Christ, may become one holy people of God.

Through Jesus Christ, your Son, Our Lord, who lives and reigns with you in the unity of the Holy Spirit, God, for ever and ever.

The people confirmed their unity with this prayer by adding their "Amen."

Charles was then vested with the chasuble and stole of a priest and Archbishop Furey anointed his hands with holy chrism.

Charles William Kram, Jr., was now a validly ordained priest of the Roman Catholic Church, forever to be known as Father Charles Kram.

He immediately proceeded to concelebrate the Mass with Archbishop Furey and the rest of the bishops and priests present.

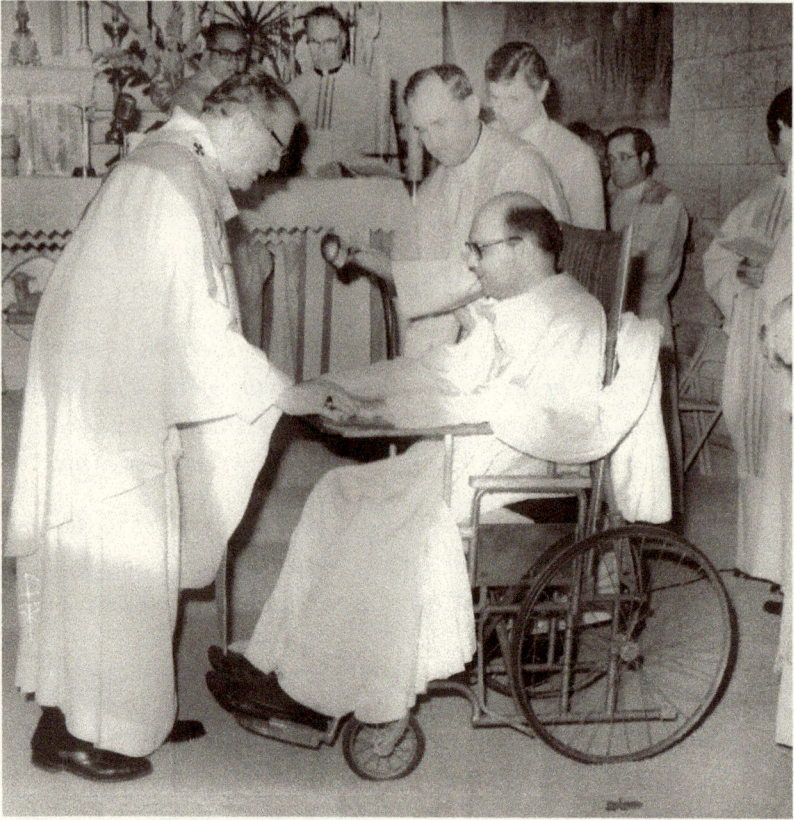

The Most Reverend Francis J. Furey, Archbishop of San Antonio, anointing the hands of the newly ordained priest, Fr. Charles W. Kram, Jr.

There can be no better commentary about the ordination than what Fr. Charles gave in his writings. Here is what we find:

The most unforgettable event in my life occurred on December 5, 1975 when at the age of forty-six I was ordained to the priesthood. An ordination is quite an event in itself, but what made mine all the more memorable was the fact that I was ordained in a wheelchair after spending half my life as a quadriplegic. I had contracted respiratory-paralytic polio in mid-1952 when I was one year shy of ordination, and under church law had been judged ineligible to continue.

Over the years numerous efforts were made to secure permission from Rome for my ordination, but the answer was always the same, "no." But in recent years the trend within the Church has been toward greater freedom and greater emphasis on love and pastoral needs than on inflexible law. Such conditions led my bishop (Archbishop Francis J. Furey, Archbishop of San Antonio, Texas) to decide in the fall of 1975 that the time for my ordination had come.

Although it was believed that His Excellency had secured permission when he was in Rome for the canonization of Elizabeth Ann Seton, he made it abundantly clear at the ordination dinner that the decision had been his and his alone and that, in my opinion, was as noteworthy as the fact of the ordination itself.

Once the decision had been made, the steps to be taken were to first ordain me a deacon and then a priest. The Archbishop appointed a committee of five priests to pay me a visit and work out the details. The visit took place on September 30, 1975, the date of my forty-sixth birthday. The diaconate was to be conferred at my home at 5 p.m. on December 4. The priestly ordination was scheduled for 2 p.m. in my parish church, Sts. Cyril and Methodius Church. My first Mass was set for 2 p.m. on Sunday, December 7 in my parish church.

October and November were extremely busy for all of us. As the weeks went by, I could feel the enthusiasm growing steadily, as details of the preparations gradually fell into place. It was much like getting ready for a wedding, except that in this case, the whole parish community was involved. In late November, a Rock and Roll combo, The Blue Diamonds, donated their talents and put on a well-attended benefit dance in my honor. It was a very gratifying gesture, especially seeing that I am more than twice the age of any one of them.

In almost no time, December arrived and the festivities began. As scheduled, on December 4 the dining room table in our home was prepared to serve as the altar. I was vested in a white alb. My mother, age eighty-two, who was now a resident in the local nursing home, had been brought home for the occasion. Also present, of course, was my father, who at the age of eighty-eight was still my faithful attendant. A few other relatives and friends also came.

Soon the Archbishop arrived in his usual jovial mood and put everyone at ease. Then Mass began, concelebrated by the Archbishop and several priests who were present. During the Mass His Excellency ordained me a deacon by the ancient rite of laying on of hands and a prayer of consecration. He also vested me with a long red stole, which as a deacon I would wear across my chest. After the ceremonies were over, we ate supper, got a good night's sleep and suddenly it was the morning of the fifth.

We had thought of spending a leisurely morning, eating a leisurely lunch, and, after a rest, departing for the church in plenty of time for the ordination. That was not to be. At 11:00 a.m., a TV newsman and his cameraman drove up for a filming and recording session. By the time they had turned off their hot lights and left, it was 12:00 noon. So, we rushed to eat, but before we had left the kitchen, we heard the voices of friends and relatives who had come to help. Soon five more men walked in. They had come in a van borrowed from a saddle factory and were ready to load me up to be transported to the church.

When our little caravan arrived at church, the red-jacketed school band was playing outside opposite the main entrance and the people had begun to arrive. We went in and after vesting in the alb and deacon's stole, I waited with my parents in the back of the church. Meanwhile, the Archbishop and three other bishops and some 100 priests who had come from near and far to take part in the ceremonies were vesting in the nearby school. At two o'clock they all came in and all but the Archbishop marched down the aisle, led by a group of white-gowned little flower girls who scattered petals in their path. Then came my parents, and finally I, followed by the Archbishop. My parents and I sat in front of the first pew as Mass began. Then my name was called and I was wheeled into the sanctuary.

As with the ordination to the diaconate, the ordination to the priesthood consists in the laying on of hands and the recitation of a prayer of consecration. Emotions ran high as the four bishops and 100 priests filed by one at a time and laid their hands on my head. The last one in line was my dear friend, Father Rudolph Hoffman, who had originally enrolled me in the seminary, and who himself now is in a wheelchair as a diabetic double amputee.

After the laying on of hands, my stole was repositioned so as to hang straight down the way a priest wears it, and I was vested in a chasuble. A chalice containing wine and a paten with a wafer of bread on it were placed on the lapboard of my chair and the four bishops and 100 priests and I proceeded to concelebrate the ordination Mass.

The ceremonies are now entirely in English, but for old time's sake, we allowed ourselves the luxury of a few old favorite Latin hymns, which brought back many happy memories of my seminary days. The youth choir did extremely well with melodies, both ancient and modern. A bearded young man later remarked that he thought he had been in heaven, and a teenage girl spoke of chills running up and down her spine. As for me, I celebrated Mass in a joyful daze.

At the end of Mass came the blessing. My first priestly blessing was for the Archbishop, who knelt before my wheelchair as I spoke the words, "May the blessing of Almighty God, the Father and the Son and the Holy Spirit, come upon you and remain with you forever." I was the ninety-eighth priest he had ordained. Then I blessed my parents, for they were so instrumental in my being there and I am so grateful to them. I said a few words to the people and prayed over them and finally gave them a blessing.

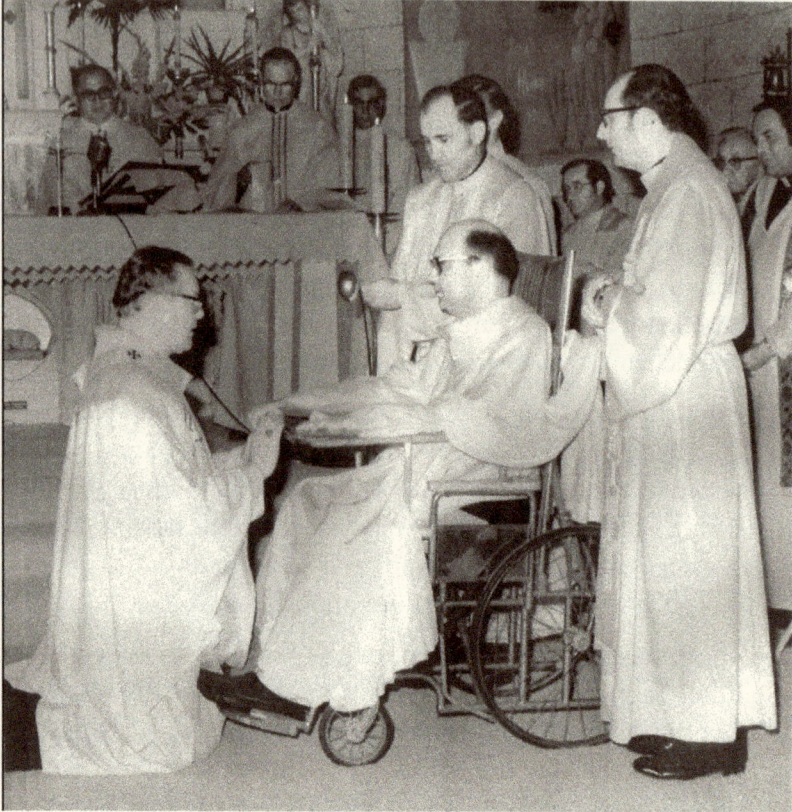

Archbishop Francis J. Furey kneeling before the newly ordained Fr. Kram for Fr. Kram's first priestly blessing.

Then the Mass was ended and, after the priests and some of the people left, I was wheeled to the center of the church to be with the crowd of well-wishers who were waiting to congratulate me.

When all the congratulations and best wishes had been accepted, it was time to proceed to the nearby parish gym where a turkey dinner was served. I ate very little that day but I did greatly appreciate being the focal point of so much happiness. There were smiles everywhere. In fact, several ladies were so carried away that they fervently kissed me. One elderly lady congratulated me at least three times. One of my teenage sweethearts whom I had not seen for almost thirty years stepped up and identified who she was. There was so much joy and love expressed that day, especially by both sides of my family that contains members of several different faith groups.

In spite of all the excitement and congratulations and praises of the day, I went to bed that night knowing very well that I was still the same old Charlie I had always been, except that now I was a priest. Oh, the love and mercy of God are beyond our expectations.

The following day, December 6, was a day of rest for us. Then came Sunday, December 7, the day of my first Mass. Compared to Friday, Sunday was relatively calm. There were no TV newsmen, no crowd in the living room, no rushing, just a leisurely van ride to church for Mass at 2 p.m.

The Mass was again concelebrated, but this time with only a handful of priests. I was the main celebrant and my good friend, Monsignor Charles Grahmann, preached the sermon. The Mass again ended with a prayer and blessing, and an invitation for everyone to attend a reception in the gym.

Monsignor Grahmann gave us these remarks about the ordination ceremony and first Mass:

On the day of ordination, Msgr. Stanley Petru pushed the wheelchair of the candidate, Reverend Mr. Charles Kram, up the aisle into the sanctuary, followed by his parents, both in wheelchairs. I pushed the wheelchair of his father as another priest pushed his mother. The church was packed with people from Shiner and the surrounding area as well as from long distances. This was an unusual moment. This is a miracle! As the bishops and the priests filed by to lay hands on Charlie's head, there wasn't a dry eye in the crowd. A dream had come true. That long awaited and anticipated day of happiness had come.

The following Sunday, Father Charles Kram celebrated his first Mass. I was privileged to give the homily for the occasion. Again, the Church in Shiner was the scene of a great crowd. Everyone, it seemed, wanted to be a part of this miracle.

It is appropriate that we present here the homily from that first Mass. It was delivered by his faithful friend, Msgr. Charles Grahmann, who had done so much to bring about this blessed event and who himself would later be elevated to the episcopacy as the first bishop of the newly formed Diocese of Victoria in Texas.

Here is that beautiful and inspiring testimony to love of God:

Father Charles Kram, Jr., Mr. and Mrs. Charles Kram, Sr., members of your family, relatives, and friends.

On Friday afternoon, many of us witnessed the ordination to the priesthood of Father Charles Kram, Jr. During that ceremony, our chief priest, Archbishop Furey, approached Charles and silently laid his hands on his head. He was followed by the imposition of hands silently of all the other bishops and priests in attendance. After that silent, solemn moment, the Archbishop prayed to God that this man, now set apart for God's work, would be a good dispenser of his graces to mankind. In that action, Charles Kram, Jr. became a priest.

Needless to say, that moment was a joyful moment. But, more joy was added to that occasion because of the circumstances that surrounded it. Charlie, as I have known him all my life, waited twenty-three years for that moment to come, hoping, maybe disappointed in its long coming, praying, sacrificing, waiting. He waited because God chose him in a special way to suffer for the building up of the Body of his Son, Jesus.

When the time was right, the Spirit of God moved the minds and hearts of many in his Church and brought to a joyful and happy conclusion this ordination to the priesthood. What a wonderful thing it is to be a part of this divinely inspired occasion.

We are all aware of the many years that Father Charles spent in his paralyzed condition. We are also aware of the two people who were intimately joined in his suffering, his mother and father. They are an inspiration to us all. Perhaps we can speak briefly about suffering and then speak further about the great event that happened to him, his ordination to the priesthood.

Recently, our Holy Father, Pope Paul VI, received in pilgrimage a large group of sick and suffering people. During the Mass he celebrated for them, Our Holy Father put into focus for all of us the place of suffering in the world. I would like to share his beautiful thoughts with you. "Here we are in your midst, beloved sons and daughters, upon whom the Lord has wished to bestow a privilege—yes, for us Christians this is a certainty, the privilege to suffer, you are thus in close communion with the mystery of the Cross of Jesus."

Pope Paul continued: "If no man is an island, if we are all united in the human family of mankind and its vocation and its history; if every soul that is elevated, elevates the whole world; if we, above all, followers of Christ and members of His Mystical Body, are united in the bond of Charity, just think what happens when such communion is realized in the offering of sufferings! Then the suffering person can repeat with the Apostles with a certain joy: 'In this mortal frame of mine, I help to pay off the debt which the afflictions of Christ still leave to be paid for the sake of His Body, the Church.' Yes, the whole Church, and with her, the whole of mankind, receives a great deal from your sorrow, transformed by the Mystery of the Cross and having become, therefore, a kind of leaven in the 'Communion of Saints.'"

Father Charles and Mr. and Mrs. Kram, your sufferings have built up all of us; you have been an example to so many of us who know you. Indeed, the whole Church is grateful to you.

Let us turn our reflections now to the priesthood. Father Charles was ordained a priest. Our Christian lives have used the services of the priest in our midst. Who is this man called a priest? Whence does he come? What is the nature of his work? There are many questions we could ask but all are about this man, the priest. Often, there is an aura of mystery about him.

The gospels tell the story of Jesus, the High Priest. But St. Paul in his Letter to the Hebrews offers us the first features of a theology of the priesthood that has as its object Christ, the one, eternal High Priest. Every priest is patterned after that first priest.

The Letter to the Hebrews was written about the year 64 and was addressed probably to ex-Jewish Christians. Living in Jerusalem, they still saw the magnificence of the Temple where the ceremonies of worship were celebrated with great solemnity. Among them was the sacrifice, with the shedding of an animal's blood, which always made a great impression and exercised a certain fascination on those present. It was an old custom, not only of Israel but of many other religions.

Saint Paul draws attention in his Letter to the Hebrews to another priest and another sacrifice; Christ, the one eternal priest, offered a different sacrifice, the one sacrifice from which the salvation of everyone is now derived.

In his preaching, Jesus had not spoken of sacrifice in a formal sense as was offered in the Temple, nor had he spoken of priesthood to the Apostles. But he had conferred on them the threefold mission of preaching the Gospel, baptizing, and remitting sins. Finally at the Last Supper, instituting the Eucharist as the sign of the continuous presence and renewal of the paschal mystery in the Church, he had asked the Apostles to carry out that work, too, to renew that last meal "in remembrance of me."

And so, the Apostles repeat what Jesus taught and did, even at the Last Supper. They institute and celebrate the breaking of the bread. They exercise the power of remitting sins, as conferred on them by Jesus, and they preach insistently that Christ is the only Savior, Redeemer, and Mediator. Saint Paul speaks of an "imposition of hands" which transmits a gift and a power entrusted by Christ to the Apostles and to the community, the same imposition we witnessed on Friday afternoon. It is a "gift of the Holy Spirit" that qualifies and designates those who receive it for specific, directive functions in the Christian community. Of himself and the Apostles, Paul says that they are "stewards of God's mysteries" and "God's assistants."

Father Charles, you are the newest steward of God's mysteries within our community. In the name of all the priests, I am happy to welcome you as a fellow priest. I welcome you as one who will continue to bring Christ into our daily lives. May God grant you many blessed and happy moments in the years of your priesthood.

It is appropriate that Msgr. Grahmann would reflect so much in his homily on the teachings of St. Paul because Father Charles relied on St. Paul for much of his strength in his weakness. On the day of his ordination, there hung in the sanctuary of Sts. Cyril and

Methodius Church a huge blue banner bearing St. Paul's words to the Corinthians, "Gladly will I glory in my infirmities."

We would do well to call to mind that it is not customary (at normal priestly ordinations) for more bishops than the consecrating bishop to exercise the gesture of laying on of hands. We recognize further that this was not a normal ordination. There is little hope that everything could be routine as we recall Fr. Kram's personal reflection on the ordination rite with his pronouncement that "Emotions ran high as four bishops and one hundred priests filed by one at a time and laid their hands on my head." And *then* Msgr. Grahmann (now the Most Reverend Charles V. Grahmann, Bishop Emeritus of Dallas) commented, as we read earlier: "This was an unusual moment. This is a miracle! As the bishops and the priests filed by to lay hands on Charlie's head, there wasn't a dry eye in the crowd. A dream had come true."

It is also interesting to note that Archbishop Furey had told Fr. Charles that he would be a counselor and consoler of the sick and afflicted and that his success in that mission would hinge on his ability to identify with the suffering since he was one of them himself.

Father Charles's ordination received very favorable and extensive coverage from *The Shiner Gazette* both leading up to the event and following it. Additional coverage was provided by the newspapers from Victoria and San Antonio as well as the Catholic press led by *Our Sunday Visitor*. Television coverage from San Antonio was also very favorable.

We would be negligent in our duty if we failed to include these important thoughts of Fr. Patrick Fidgeon as reported in *The Shiner Gazette* on November 27, 1975. In commenting on the upcoming ordination of Charles Kram, Fr. Fidgeon stated:

> We pray that the spiritual significance of the ordination of Rev. Charles Kram will be seen by all. In his own wonderful way, Almighty God is bestowing a great blessing on our parish, our community, and our Archdiocese. God will use this occasion to teach all of us many lessons.

The dignity of the priesthood, its place in God's salvation plan, its importance to God's people, are all messages that will be relayed to us. At a time in the Church when we need a return to spiritual values, an increase in the understanding of life, its meaning and purpose, the story of Charles Kram will have tremendous impact.

We must never forget that these years of waiting have been spent by Charles in many ways, mostly spiritual ways. These have been years of prayers, years of offering to God his patient suffering. His ordination brings news of all this, and the news brings inspiration to all of us.

Charles Kram's life has been a great example of loving resignation to God's Will. One must recognize too the great devotion over the years of his father and mother, his brother and sister. They have cared for him. They have shared with him his waiting, his pain, his loneliness. Without them, his difficult life would have been more difficult, if not impossible. May God bless them.

A very fitting and beautiful message from the newly ordained Father Charles Kram to all the people of God was printed in the Sts. Cyril and Methodius Church bulletin dated December 14, 1975. His message was:

Dear Friends, Many a tear was shed in our parish last weekend, but such tears were never more acceptable, because they were tears of joy. The goodness of God truly has no end. I wish each one of you could have taken my place for just a moment, to feel the happiness you brought me. Your joy and enthusiasm were wonderful to behold and God was surely much honored by it all. If I live to be a hundred, I know I will still rejoice in the happy memory of those two perfect days. I thank God for good health and good weather and much more. But most of all, I thank God for you. I love you all, and I assure you that none of you will ever be without a priest to intercede for you and your loved ones before the Throne of God. Please do not forget to pray for me.

Seated left to right, Fr. Charles Kram and his mother, Emma Zander Kram.

Standing left to right, Edgar Kram (brother), Charles Kram, Sr. (father), and Felicia Kram Argubright (sister).

Photo was taken at the reception following Fr. Kram's priestly ordination on December 5, 1975.

CHAPTER SIX

In Persona Christi Capitis

The teachings of the Catholic Church are contained in the *Catechism of the Catholic Church* as promulgated by St. John Paul II. In paragraph 1548, we read this:

> In the ecclesial service of the ordained minister, it is Christ himself who is present to his Church as Head of his Body, Shepherd of his flock, High Priest of the redemptive sacrifice, Teacher of Truth. This is what the Church means by saying that the priest, by virtue of the sacrament of Holy Orders, acts "in persona Christi Capitis." It is the same priest, Christ Jesus, whose sacred person his minister represents. Now the minister, by reason of his sacerdotal consecration that he has received, is truly made to be like the high priest and possesses the authority to act in the power and place of the person of Christ himself. Christ is the source of all priesthood: the priest of the old law was a figure of Christ and the priest of the new law acts in the person of Christ.

Father Charles clearly understood the objective of his ordination. God had not elevated him to the order of a priest simply to satisfy his personal longing to be a priest. After all, he had always wanted to be a priest only because that was the way to answer God's call for him to serve God as God willed it to be. It was God's will that Charles become a priest so he could serve in the manner that God chose.

It was as if Charles had, all his life, seen God searching for someone to share the suffering of all the people who hurt in any way and Charles had responded in the fashion of Isaiah: "Here I am, Lord, send me." And so, God set the world in motion much as a line of dominoes are set to influence the next one to move. Thus Charles, the suffering quadriplegic who longed to serve God in whatever way God chose, was now Fr. Charles who was empowered to minister to the people in the person of Christ.

Monsignor Charles Grahmann, when he was speaking at Fr. Kram's first Mass, made these observations on the priesthood. He explained that the functions of a priest are threefold, as follows:

> First, the proclamation of God's Word and the proclamation of redemption. This is particularly the task of the Apostles, their collaborators and successors, the priests, to preach God's Word and proclaim his redemption. Second, the reconciliation of man with God by means of the remission of sins, which take place in Baptism, in Penance, and in the other sacraments. Third, the building up of the Body of Christ, the Church, the joint work of all believers, but in which the apostle (the priest) is, as it were, an architect. In all of this work, it is wholly evident that the true Master Priest and Head of the Church is the one and only Jesus Christ. The other priests are his Vicars or Assistants.

He went on to explain that a priest is a man with a human dimension as well as a sacred dimension. In the human dimension, he possesses all the qualities and defects, all the strengths and weaknesses, all the robustness and frailties, all the feelings, passions, ideals, and needs of his human nature. In that regard, a priest experiences all the challenges in life that we all experience. By virtue of his educational and environmental influences, he is often strengthened in his ability to handle many of these challenges. In his sacred dimension, the priest is brought closer to God, through the concept of consecration, than the laity generally are. As a man dedicated to and ordained for service to God and mankind, he is influenced to focus his attention toward God's Way and away from man's way.

This consecration that he experiences is for the service of others, rather than of himself. It is designed to direct his attention toward God and neighbor and away from his personal interests.

Early in his priesthood ministry, Fr. Charles reflected on what his ministry was like. He observed that on the day of his ordination, Archbishop Furey had predicted he would be a counselor and consoler of the sick and afflicted since he was one of them and he could easily identify with them. He described his ministry as being mainly one of sharing the burdens of others. Many persons had telephoned and written asking for prayers and blessings. Others contacted him to share their happy or lonely thoughts or to offer a bit of poetry. He was encouraged by the many who came to him for face-to-face confession and to receive the forgiveness of their sins.

He was pleasantly surprised by the continuous flow of requests for Masses. He celebrated Mass in his room at home several times a week when a fellow priest or the nuns from Shiner would come to assist him.

Celebrating Mass presented unique challenges for him. The archbishop had granted him the privilege of celebrating Mass while seated since he was unable to stand. He had also received special permission to use assistants who handled the wafer of bread and the chalice of wine for the most solemn part of the Mass, the consecration of the Eucharist. These assistants were either clergy or consecrated religious persons or laity who had been commissioned by the Church to act as Extraordinary Ministers of Communion. These assistants also assisted him by vesting him and arranging things on the altar and turning the pages of the Missal and whatever other functions required the use of the hands. Through the use of the slings and braces rigged up on his wheelchair, he was able to perform a limited number of hand movements and especially to make the Sign of the Cross.

He continued his Ham radio ministry that reached other operators all over the world. He was particularly effective in reaching out to many other operators who were also shut-ins like him who had limited outside contacts due to similar circumstances. His counseling and consoling and praying ministry grew in spiritual value as more and more of his contacts learned of his remarkable priestly ordination in spite of his handicaps. This unimaginable occurrence alone brought hope to many other sufferers, hope that they, too, might be able to achieve their dreams and purposes in life.

Coupling his radio ministry with his CUSAN ministry was a natural marriage. With his priestly ordination, Father Charles assumed the role of spiritual advisor of his tape group in CUSA.

You might recall reading in Chapter Four that CUSA is an organization of people with a chronic illness or disability who assist each other to bear their suffering in union with Christ on the Cross. They are devoted to sharing their joy of being close to Christ by way of their suffering. Their motto is: *We suffer for a purpose*. What a beautiful thought that is. Just think of the many people who waste their suffering by feeling sorry for themselves. What a tragedy that is.

Very soon after his ordination, the archdiocese, in cooperation with the priests of the area, purchased a van suitably revised to meet his needs. It contained a hydraulic lift for his wheelchair plus proper safety devices to secure his chair in place while the vehicle was in motion. This thoughtful gesture on the part of his fellow priests and the archdiocese was greatly appreciated. It served his transportation needs for many years.

It is interesting to learn that his ordination in such a disabled physical condition presented some questions regarding his ability to validly administer the sacraments of the Church. For example, with the limited use of his hands, how could he anoint the baptized and the sick with the sacred oils? It was deemed that a properly commissioned person could act as his hands while Fr. Charles pronounced the formula of prayers. In the spirit of solving all problems, it turned out that since the Holy Spirit, acting through the Church officials, had approved his ordination, it was possible to find solutions to all the upcoming obstacles or questions. We will see the overwhelming truth of this fact later in this story when tragedy strikes and Fr. Charles's father (his primary caregiver) dies.

For now, though, suffice it to say that the Spirit of God is definitely in charge.

With Fr. Charles's mother in the nursing home, his father had become his sole caregiver. Mr. Kram was now in his upper eighties and doing all the farm chores and caregiver chores by himself was taking its toll on his health.

We know from life's own lessons that God provides for our needs. At a time when Mr. Kram needed help the most, a young nurse who was married and the mother of two learned of his need and responded. It is not beyond reason to feel that Delores Hrncir heard God calling for a helper and, much like Isaiah, replied, "Here I am, Lord, send me."

There were few people in the area more occupied than Delores. She and her husband, Marcus, operated a dairy near town. That in itself is a full-time job. In addition to her role as wife, mother, dairy hand and nurse, she now went to the Kram residence every day to assist Mr. Kram with much of the caregiver's duties. Sometimes she was able to get her friend, Mary Rose Barta, who worked in the Church office, to accompany her. Delores's family supported her fully in these efforts. In fact, she tells how her husband often accompanied her to the Kram residence after they milked their cows and delivered the milk to town and took the children (daughter Carol and son Marc) to school. While she attended to Fr. Charles's medical and hygienic needs, her husband helped Mr. Kram with the barnyard chores. Often she brought meals from their home to the Kram residence since Mr. Kram was not what one would call an accomplished cook.

Father Pat Fidgeon was pastor of Sts. Cyril and Methodius Church at the time. He acknowledged their dedication to helping Fr. Charles and his dad in their needs. We will see later how critical that dedication was.

Father Charles spent the time in prayer and in writing when he wasn't ministering to his world-wide congregation on his Ham radio. Writing was an important outlet for his thoughts and reflections. We are fortunate to have much of what he wrote. We will cite here some examples of those reflections.

PRAYER WITH FAITH

To everyone who believes in the power of prayer:

So much harm is done by worry and doubt and so much good is done by faith and by prayer backed up by a strong faith. Anyone can be a prophet of doom but anyone can also be a prophet of prosperity and of good days ahead. Prophesies of either kind tend to be self-fulfilling because they affect our way of thinking and of acting and of spreading our feelings and they certainly affect the strength of our faith.

Peter walked on water until he doubted. Then he sank. Jesus was disappointed in him and asked him why he faltered. If we doubt, we sink (Matthew 14:22-33).

Once when a Canaanite woman asked Jesus for a favor, he said no, because she was an outsider and it wouldn't be right to throw the children's food to the dogs. So the woman asked for table scraps. Her faith and perseverance pleased Jesus so much that he promptly granted her request, assuring her that the evil spirit had already left her sick little child (Matthew 15:21-28).

Where Jesus is concerned we are by no means outsiders. We belong to him more than any other people could and we have a high claim on his favors, provided that we have faith. Faith is so important that the miracle working powers of Jesus were seriously hindered in his own native place for no other reason than that the people there did not believe in him. Faith could have brought his own people their full share of wonders (Mark 6:1-6).

James says that we must ask in faith, never doubting, and that the doubter must not expect to receive anything from the Lord (James 2:14-17).

Faith is also a gift to be asked for, so first pray for a strong faith. Then pray as one filled with the joyful expectation that the answer is already on the way. Crowd out every fear or doubt or negative thought with something positive and encouraging and make a strong reaffirmation of faith, like, "Everything will turn out all right," or "Lord, I used to doubt, but not any more."

To ask as if we wish to receive implies that the less we ask, the less we will receive. God is lavish with his gifts, but he wants to be asked. Ask a great deal.

Worrying indicates a lack of faith and accomplishes nothing useful. In fact, why should the worrier ever bother to pray? A man once complained to God and asked him why he was taking so long to answer his prayers. God told him, "My child, I couldn't help you because you just wouldn't let go."

It has been said that one thing that we, God's children, owe to our beloved Father is not ever to be afraid of anything. "Do not be afraid, little flock, for the Father has been pleased to give you the Kingdom" (Luke 12:32).

A simple prayer that anyone can say over and over throughout the day is, "Jesus, I love you." This simple expression of love can be given as many meanings as there are feelings in the human heart: "I love you," "I let go," "I abandon myself to you," "I'm sad today and I just wanted you to know," "I'll hang on until you rescue me."

Instead of worrying then, let's all ask our Father for a strong faith, then let's pray with a firm faith, do it often and do it without faltering. Any time and every time you feel a worry or a doubt or a cloud of gloom coming on, quickly say, "Jesus, I love you." You will be heard.

Here is another example of his thoughts:

OUR PURPOSE IN LIFE

We each have our own identity. We are each distinct from one another. We will each always be who we always are. Discovering the real you in each of us can be difficult because a human being can be very complicated. We human beings tend to be like onions, made up of many layers of outward appearances. Peeling off the layers one by one in an effort to find the real you sometimes shows that once the layers are all removed, there is little left.

Feelings of doubt and uncertainty are a part of everyone's life. Take the question of job security, for example. Drilling rigs shut down, drought ruins the cattle business, companies downsize. A livelihood that seems secure today may disappear tomorrow.

Just recently a well-paid friend of mine told me that he had been made to take a $13,000-a-year cut in pay which changed his long-term financial plans completely.

If you have a sweetheart or spouse today, you may find yourself alone tomorrow.

On the health scene, it has been predicted that if the AIDS epidemic is not checked, 100 million will die from it by the year 2000. There are now more than 150 known strains of the AIDS virus. For polio, there were only three.

Jesus said, "He who seeks only himself brings himself to ruin." He also said: "He who brings himself to naught for me discovers who he is" (Matthew 10:38–39).

So how can we avoid seeking ourselves too much and discover who we are?

First, we can try always to cultivate a good attitude. A friend of mine suffered a back injury in a wreck several years ago and since then has never been without pain. She could be angry and bitter but she is not. Her attitude is, "At least I can feel." She has taught herself to ignore the pain and keep going. In fact, she works two jobs in order to get her children through school. The secret to her success is her attitude. In fact, it is said that success is 90% attitude and only 10% effort. Is your attitude helping you or is it hurting you? What will you do to change it?

By the way, did you know that picante sauce is nothing but ketchup with a bad attitude?

Secondly, we can help by trying to bring out the best in others. As a young man, I learned a poem that said, "Full many a flower is born to blush unseen and waste its fragrance on the desert air" (Elegy Written in a Church Yard by Thomas Gray 1716-1771). That poem illustrates the fact that many talents can lie unused unless someone discovers them and brings them out.

We can help bring out the best in others by judging them, not by their outward appearance but by the contents of their minds and hearts.

An excellent example of this is the little group of Eucharistic Ministers who help me with the Mass. When I asked for help, they said such things as, "I'm not worthy," or "I'm too clumsy," or "I can't read well." But once they had done it successfully, their hesitancy disappeared. They rose to the challenge because they were asked. Do you know someone you could help simply by encouraging them?

Thirdly, we must let God lead us. God is unpredictable. His plan is eternal and sometimes takes strange and unexpected turns and we do not know where he may want to lead us next. If we accept each day as a new calling from him, we will soon discover that one day's stumbling block may be another day's stepping stone and that often God closes one door so that he may open another one. Many a coincidence turns out to be a next step.

So let's not live in fear of tomorrow. God is already there. How exciting it is to wonder what our next calling will be. If he calls us, he will also provide the means.

In summary, we can avoid seeking ourselves too much and discover who we are by cultivating a good attitude, by helping others to achieve their purpose in life and by giving God our full trust.

Here is his reflection on suffering and who, we ask, could possibly have a better understanding of suffering? This is outstanding!

SUFFERING—WHAT GOOD IS IT?

No one can honestly say, "I never suffer." The world is full of sufferings of every kind. Even newborn babies suffer. The first thing that happens to them as soon as they are born is that they get spanked by the doctor, but some say that they cry immediately because they are born with their share of our huge national debt. But, all joking aside, why do innocent babies suffer?

Actually, there is much about suffering that is a mystery. The Bible often mentions it but offers no final solution. In general, suffering is the result of sin. That is, if Adam and Eve had not sinned, we would not have to suffer.

But in an individual case, we can't connect an individual's suffering with his sins, unless we mean such natural consequence as emphysema from smoking or liver disease from drinking or AIDS from sharing infected drug needles.

The famous atheist, Madalyn Murray O'Hare, once said that she couldn't believe that God exists because if he did, there couldn't be such things as deformed babies and earthquakes and storms.

Can God will evil? God cannot will moral evil, that is, God cannot will sin. Approving of sin would be impossible to his nature as God. But he can permit it. We are living proof of that.

God can will physical evils such as earthquakes and floods and giant meteors striking the earth. These result from the working out of the laws of nature established by God. If they happen when they should, we thank God for a miracle.

Why, then, does God so often let the innocent suffer while the guilty prosper? One preacher answered this question by saying that it is because God does not balance his books once a month like accountants do, but that one day there will be a day of reckoning.

Another and perhaps better answer would be the fact that God uses suffering to bring about great good. Think of how the suffering of his innocent Son brought about the defeat of Satan and of sin and death and the redemption of the world.

Saint Paul endured countless sufferings for the sake of Christ—stoning, imprisonment, shipwreck, constant persecution. His attitude was, as he said to his people, "I rejoice now in the sufferings I bear for your sake, and in my flesh I am filling up what is lacking in the afflictions of Christ on behalf of his body, which is the Church" (Colossians 1:24).

As long as we live in this world, suffering will remain with us. Our clinics and hospitals and treatment centers are special places for people who are suffering, and anyone who visits or works there soon sees how much a part of human life suffering is, but also in the school and in the home, in the store and in the church, in the park and on the street, everywhere, the story is the same.

As Christians, though, we need not despair. One day our suffering will be over, and when in heaven, we see God face to face, we will see why everything we had to go through here had to be the way it was and we will rejoice exceedingly.

Then it will no longer be important whether we were rich or poor, a success or a failure, healthy or not. What will matter then is whether our trials made us bitter or better, sinners or saints. The choice is ours.

As Christians, then, rather than question God or become angry with him, we take care of ourselves as best we can.

We ask God for his help. We accept what we have and we trust God and his mysterious ways for the rest.

Lord Jesus, thank you for consoling us in our sufferings and being always our example and our strength. Help us to accept our sufferings patiently and to achieve their purpose to the fullest. Grant that by our willing endurance we may one day join you in the glory your sufferings won for us. Amen.

Another excellent expression of his thoughts is expressed here on the subject of self-giving to God.

GIVING ONESELF TO GOD

When a man and wife have a fight, the traditional way of making up is for the husband to bring her candy or flowers. Actually, giving someone a gift can express almost any kind of sentiment: "I love you," "I thank you," "I'm sorry," and so on. Primitive people offered gifts to their gods, to turn away their anger, to gain their favor, to atone for sins, and to show their submission. Many sacrifices of lambs and bulls and food were offered in this way.

When Jesus died on the cross, he was the one who offered the sacrifice. He was the victim. He offered himself freely as the Lamb of God who takes away the sins of the world. When he died for us, it was a case of giving himself.

When Jesus praised the poor widow for giving everything she had, he was saying that it isn't what you give, or the amount, but why you give is what is important. The widow's small gift was so precious because it amounted to her livelihood and, as such, was a gift of her very being, a free and generous sacrifice (Luke 21:1–4).

When you see an opportunity to give something, your time, your work, your cash, or anything else, it's your attitude that counts. Why not do it with an attitude like this: "This isn't just something I have that I am giving, but I give a bit of myself away, and I do it to please the Lord and to do for others as the Lord has so generously done for me"?

Prayer: *Lord Jesus, thank you for being so generous to me. Help me to be generous to others. Grant that my gift may inspire many others to work and sacrifice for you. Amen.*

There is another fascinating side to the story of this remarkable man.

Sister Elaine Braden, IWBS, recalled that Fr. Kram never displayed any signs of dwelling on his disability. Instead, he focused on the positive aspects of his life.

Another nun concurred. She said that this was so evident when she and the other nuns brought school children to visit him as a work of corporal mercy. When they came to bring him their love and support, he gave them joy and instruction on how to use the gifts God has given to us. They were always fascinated by the way he could use a stick held in his mouth to type a letter and to draw cartoons that he would then give to them. Sometimes he would paint a picture in the same way or show them how he used his radio to communicate with someone on the other side of the world. He often did card tricks for them or told funny stories. She said they always came away marveling at how positive he made life seem even though he was so severely handicapped. Then, to top off the delight of the visit, he always sent the children a letter thanking them for their thoughtfulness.

It was his nature to direct his attention on his visitors rather than on himself.

John Butschek, whose wife Mary did so much to gather the information on Fr. Charles's life, summed up just about all we can say about Fr. Charles. He said, "I didn't know St. Joseph personally, but I would compare Fr. Kram and St. Joseph. He lived his life to fulfill God's purpose for him."

What a beautiful testimony that is.

CHAPTER SEVEN

Tragedy Strikes

Have no anxiety at all, but in everything, by prayer and petition, with thanksgiving, make your requests to God. Then the peace of God that surpasses all understanding will guard your hearts and minds in Christ Jesus. (Philippians 4:6–7)

It was Thursday, February 24, 1977. Mr. Kram went about his chores on the farm while Fr. Charles was in the wheelchair he operated by moving a lever with his chin.

One of the annual projects for this time of the year on the Kram farm was burning the bamboo grass at one edge of the property. This grass grew tall and the stems made great fishing poles and stakes for garden plants, but it was also very invasive and required vigorous control measures. The annual burn was Mr. Kram's primary control tactic. He set the grass on fire and stayed with it to contain it and prevent its spreading.

Some details of exactly what happened will never be known, but Mr. Kram apparently was overcome by smoke inhalation as the wind shifted and he collapsed into the fire. His clothing caught fire and he was unable to recover.

Father Charles was alone at home and was unable to move from his wheelchair. He could not see what was happening, but he sensed that something bad had happened to his father and he was unable to do anything about it. He prayed for help.

Someone in the neighborhood noticed that the fire was out of control and alerted the Shiner Fire Department, and it immediately dispatched a fire truck and crew to the scene.

Pastor Travis A. Rider, Jr., who is presently retired, but in 1977 was the pastor of the First United Methodist Church in Shiner, heard about the fire from the Fire Department. He rushed out to the Kram farm and arrived right behind the Fire Department personnel. He described the scene for us.

He was a close friend of Fr. Charles and his parents, having visited with Fr. Charles on numerous occasions. When he arrived at the Kram residence, the smoke was very thick and covered much of the area. He reached the house and found Fr. Charles in his wheelchair on the front porch. Father Charles was actively concerned for his father's safety because he was frail and he was eighty-nine years old, and it appeared that the fire was out of control. Father Charles told Pastor Rider of his concerns. Pastor Rider drove to the scene of the fire and was almost overcome by the smoke, but he felt he must find Mr. Kram. Working his way through the area, he located the firemen and together they searched for Mr. Kram. Soon they found his badly burned body where he had fallen into the fire.

One of the firemen called for an ambulance and the local Justice of the Peace, while Pastor Rider returned to the residence. It was his difficult duty to tell Fr. Charles that his father was dead. Together they went into the house and prayed.

Ordained ministers of God are often confronted with tragedy and the need to comfort and console family members, but this was particularly difficult. The Kram family was more like family than friends to him. The two clergymen consoled and comforted each other as they prayed for God's mercy and accepted God's will.

The local Justice of the Peace, Mrs. Jo A. Pruitt, held an inquest and judged that his death was an accident that occurred about 4:00 p.m.

News of the tragedy spread quickly throughout the community. Soon Fr. Pat Fidgeon heard what happened. He knew he had to act swiftly since Fr. Charles would be left by himself and certainly would need help. He drove out to the Marcus and Delores

Hrncir dairy and told them what happened. He told Delores to gather an overnight bag of things she would need and to accompany him to the Kram residence as she would have to stay with Fr. Charles to care for him until some arrangements for his care could be made. Neither he nor she nor anyone in the family knew how long that would be. Her husband and two children understood and approved of her involvement.

When Fr. Pat and Mrs. Hrncir arrived at the Kram residence, they found that Edgar Kram was there caring for his brother. They were consoling each other as brothers would do in a case like this.

Needless to say, Fr. Charles was grateful for his brother's presence and support. He was most grateful for Delores Hrncir's presence. She was a nurse, a caregiver, and, most importantly, she was a trusted friend with whom he was comfortable. She took over the duty of caring for him.

Even so, the night of February 24, 1977, was the most difficult night of his life.

His dear mother was in the nursing home, and he could not be with her to console her and comfort her. He could not also benefit from her soothing motherly words of wisdom. His dear father who had always been his strongest supporter and caregiver was now gone to eternity. As a Christian, we find great consolation in the belief that death is not the end of our life; it is really the beginning of the most important part of our existence. Yet as we rejoice over a loved one's entry into eternity, we grieve for our loss. Losing a loved one is often the single most painful moment in our life. Father Charles reminded himself of the glorious celebration that must be taking place in heaven with his father's arrival there. Surely God must have said to him, "Well done, my good and faithful servant. Come, share your master's joy" (Matthew 25:23). Father Charles realized he must deal with his own issues. His brother and sister, both of whom he loved very much and who loved him as well, each had their own family issues with which to deal. Yet it was important that he do what he could to console them in their grief.

He prayed to Mary, the Mother of God, for guidance and strength and wisdom. "What will happen to me now?" was a major concern, not so much for his own personal comfort and peace of mind, but "what about the mission that God has given to me?" "I have not yet done the work that God sent me to do and I need help so I can accomplish that. Please help me do what I must do." He prayed and he prayed.

He expressed his concerns to Delores. In her wisdom, she urged him to simply "trust God to provide for your needs."

It was a simple solution. "You prayed to become a priest and God provided the means. You prayed for help when you sensed that your dad was in trouble and God sent help. Trust God to provide for your care so you can go about the work God has for you," she counseled. "What did Jesus say about being concerned about our well-being? Look at the birds in the sky. Do you see them worrying?" she said. It's no wonder he felt comfortable with her around.

Sometimes the simplest solutions to our problems seem to be the most complicated. "Have Faith"; "Trust in God"; "He will provide." What can be less complicated than that?

Funeral services, arranged by the family, were set for 10:00 a.m. on Saturday, February 26 with Fr. Charles as the main celebrant at the Mass. Twenty-four other priests participated as concelebrants. Monsignor Charles Grahmann was chosen by the family to deliver the homily.

Immediately after the death of Mr. Kram, Fr. Patrick Fidgeon and Msgr. Charles Grahmann, independently of each other, went to work seeking a place for Fr. Charles to reside.

The Sisters of the Incarnate Word and Blessed Sacrament in Victoria, Texas, owned and operated the Huth Memorial Hospital in nearby Yoakum. They had repeatedly petitioned the Archdiocese of San Antonio for a priest to be assigned to the hospital as chaplain, but none was ever available.

Now the work of the two priests intersected like a gift from heaven. In exchange for Fr. Charles being assigned as hospital chaplain, the hospital agreed to give him a place to live and to provide for his daily care. It was like a marriage made in heaven.

The hospital staff and the patients welcomed him with open arms and he was grateful for the care, but mostly for the opportunity to serve God and his people.

Didn't Archbishop Furey predict at Fr. Charles's ordination that he would be counselor and consoler of the sick and disabled and that he would be able to relate to them since he is one of them?

God *does* provide.

It was as if God spoke the words of 2 Corinthians 12:9 to Fr. Charles: "My grace is sufficient for you, for my power is made perfect in weakness."

God's way may sometimes seem strange to us mortals, but that's because we think as humans think and not as God thinks.

Chapter Eight

Hospital Chaplain

I asked God for strength, that I might achieve;

I was made weak, that I might learn humbly to obey.

I asked for health, that I might do greater things;

I was given infirmity, that I might do better things.

I asked for riches, that I might be happy;

I was given poverty, that I might be wise.

I asked for power, that I might have the praise of men;

I was given weakness, that I might feel the need of God.

I asked for all things, that I might enjoy life;

I was given life, that I might enjoy all things.

I got nothing I asked for, but everything I hoped for.

Almost despite myself, my unspoken prayers were answered.

I am among all men most richly blessed.

(This prayer is said to have been found in the pocket of a dead Confederate soldier after the July 2, 1863, battle at Devil's Den on the Gettysburg Battlefield. The prayer is generally known as "A Confederate Soldier's Prayer" and the soldier's name is unknown. It has been adopted by many in the field of rehabilitation as "A Creed for the Disabled.")

On March 9, 1977, the Most Reverend Francis J. Furey, Archbishop of San Antonio, formally appointed Fr. Charles Kram chaplain of Huth Memorial Hospital in Yoakum, Texas. This formality made official that which had already taken place.

Delores and Marcus Hrncir had moved Fr. Charles from the family farm to Huth Memorial Hospital on Sunday evening, February 27, 1977, in anticipation of the chaplaincy being made official as soon as the appointment could be finalized.

Huth Memorial Hospital was built in 1922 with money from a local bond issue and money donated for a hospital by the late John Huth. At the time of its beginning, the hospital had thirteen beds and all the modern services.

The City of Yoakum operated the hospital until June 12, 1933, when management was assumed by the Sisters of the Incarnate Word and Blessed Sacrament. When Fr. Charles joined the hospital as chaplain, there were thirteen nuns in various capacities ranging from administrator to nurses and aides. In time the hospital grew to a capacity of fifty-five patients and ninety-eight employees; many were members of the Catholic religious order, but the majority were civilians.

One of those ninety-eight employees was Hazel Pfeil, a nurse who retired after thirty-eight years of caring for the sick, wounded, disabled, newborn, and dying people of the area. In an interview with Mary Butschek on March 18, 2005, she told about her relationship with Fr. Charles. Mary Butschek's record of that interview is an interesting story in itself. Here is that story:

> Hazel Pfeil was a nurse for thirty-eight years in the Yoakum Hospital even though she was not a Catholic; in fact, she belonged to the Baptist Church. She had known Fr. Kram since childhood as they were only one year apart in age. Hazel was on duty when he arrived at the hospital shortly after his father's tragic death. She recalls that Father did not know what would happen to him until the opportunity of being hospital chaplain arose. The arrangement was beneficial for him and the hospital as the Sisters wanted a chaplain and he needed expert and constant care. Father

was grateful to the Sisters and he and the Sisters helped each other in many ways. As chaplain, Father was always nearby and he could usually be found near the emergency room or waiting rooms to visit and comfort the patients and their families.

"He was so kind and compassionate," said Hazel. "Everyone could see that Father knew pain and suffering and he had been down the road that they were enduring, and he gave them a spiritual uplift. He was a blessing to the hospital."

"He was always priestly in his manner and he was always dressed in his Roman collar. He wore his crown well," Hazel said, adding, "When you were around him, *you* felt holy." Her evaluation is that "[p]erhaps, he was a saint all his life."

When asked if she ever saw Father angry, Hazel said, "No. Never. He may have sometimes been frustrated, but not angry. If he felt angry, he kept it to himself."

To the question, "Did you ever see Father despondent?" Hazel's observation was, "I'm sure he must have gotten despondent, but you know what, I think he would say a little extra prayer and he would overcome it. But *I* definitely felt it *for* him because when I put myself in that position, I don't know if I would want to live."

Some of the special joys of Father's life were his yearly "surprise" birthday parties that the hospital staff threw for him. "He looked forward and appreciated them like a kid and would have been very disappointed if we had not had a party" was Hazel's opinion.

Before coming to the hospital, Father had celebrated Mass in his home with only a few people present, but when he celebrated Mass in the hospital chapel, there were always dedicated people who usually attended daily. Hazel remembered, "There were several little old ladies who couldn't walk very well, but they were there each afternoon for Father's Mass," and his Sunday Masses were always well attended. Visitors, friends, staff, and all who came in contact with Father were amazed at what an outstanding man he was as he moved around the hospital and used the stick in his mouth to open and operate the elevator or to go outside to greet anyone entering the hospital. "He was our greeter," Hazel said with a smile.

His extraordinary memory impressed those close to him and also those who helped him by opening his mail and other little tasks. He knew exactly into which box or manila folder each piece of paper or other object belonged. Each folder was numbered, and he was meticulous about having everything where it should be and in perfect order. As time went on, his strength slowly and gradually waned, and Hazel said that to the last, Father would be taken out of bed later in the day because he got very uncomfortable sitting for long times. In the final years, it was in the afternoon before he was put into his chair. His bed was a rocking bed that continually see-sawed to help him breathe and to keep his lungs clear of mucous. When his bed was not rocking, Father was on a respirator. During his waking hours of lying in bed unable to move any part of his body (except for his head), Father would listen to inspirational audiotapes in which he seemed to find great comfort.

"He was truly loved by many, many people and he touched lives in very special ways. Father was a holy man who is very deserving of being canonized a saint," said Father's faithful friend and caregiver, Hazel Pfeil.

Another interesting reflection on her relationship with Fr. Charles and his life as a hospital chaplain comes from Karen Fikac Roznovsky, who knew him for many years:

> I began working at Huth Memorial Hospital in April 1980. I don't remember any startling moment or anything like that about meeting Fr. Kram for the first time—in his wheelchair and his way of breathing, bobbing his head, which I have been told is referred to as "frog breathing." I probably didn't react because I knew of him as a student at St. Ludmila's Academy in Shiner and from the major celebration of his ordination in 1975 when I was thirteeen years old. However, I feel it was more than that. It was just the way he had of greeting a person and putting them at ease that helped me see beyond his handicap and to see him

as a person, as a priest, as a very holy man. From that day forward, I considered him a friend and an ally.

Father Kram was the same age as my dad. They were born only one month apart in 1929. When dad was a patient in the hospital, he looked forward to visits from Fr. Kram. I know they would pray privately and then again when we were in the room with them. I don't know what they talked about but I know they respected each other very much. Dad suffered from asthma as a child and later in life from COPD and congestive heart failure. He and Fr. Kram were "two of a kind" in that they did not dwell on their illnesses and went about life as normally as possible. They both battled illnesses throughout their lives, but still lived past seventy years. Father Kram died on August 13, 2000, and Dad died on August 13, 2002, exactly two years later. My family took that as a good sign. It was comforting to know that the two long-time friends were united even in death.

Father Kram thoroughly enjoyed his birthday celebrations. Every year, the hospital staff would throw a party for him. He was all smiles and he would say, "You all shouldn't have." It's funny that one year when he said, "Ya'll shouldn't have," someone apparently took him seriously as we did not have a party the next year. I remember how sad he looked and, of course, we all noticed, and so he didn't say that anymore and we continued to have birthday celebrations for him thereafter.

I remember being a very new employee in the business office on the first floor of the old hospital and working the noon to 8 p.m. shift. I would leave the door to the office open to the hallway so that when Father came by in his wheelchair, we could talk and I could help him, if needed. The emergency room, radiology department, pharmacy, laboratory, surgery suite, central supply, dietary department, chapel, and the dining room with vending machines were on the first floor. Sometimes, especially on weekends or holidays, it would get very quiet and lonely, so Father's visits were something to which I looked forward. All other patient care was on the second and third floors. Father would always be most apologetic for "bothering" me, but really he was no bother. He would ask for help with various things like making copies on the copy machine. I remember once when I made a copy, there was some of the liquid paper we used at the time that had stuck to the glass on the machine and Father instructed me regarding how to clean it. As I said, I was pretty new to office work at the time. I distinctly remember Father telling me that if he could, that would be one thing that he would always make sure that the copier machine glass was squeaky clean because that way everyone would get good clean copies every time. I remember thinking, at the time, what a small matter that was in the grand scheme of things and yet here was this man who desired to do such a small thing that to him was so important, if only he were able to do it. This was something that I took for granted, that I could do these things.

Any time we were alerted that an ambulance was approaching the hospital, word would be sent to Father and he would get to the emergency room as fast as he could in case he was needed. He would never get in the way of the medical personnel, but he stayed nearby to anoint the patient when appropriate and to console the family and friends if needed.

Over the years, I would help Fr. Kram with various paperwork, mailings, etc., always following his very thorough and patient instructions. Father was always encouraging. He was so patient. He always had time for the employees, patients, and visitors.

I remember conversations we had where Father would make suggestions to solve various issues. As I worked in the administration department, Father liked to bend my ear from time to time. He usually had good ideas about how to make things and processes work better. Sometimes I was able to help him get his ideas across to administration and sometimes I could not. It wasn't something he asked me to do, but I would mention things when I could. I'm sure he noticed changes when they did occur, but we did not discuss them. He wasn't seeking credit for any of his ideas. I think he just found joy in seeing things going more smoothly.

Father loved to park his wheelchair just outside the front door of the hospital on nice days and greet people as they came and left. Things I remember doing for Father were just everyday things like adjusting his shawl when he was cold, adjusting his cup and straw so he could drink, putting some treat on his plate at a gathering in just the right place so he could feed himself, re-positioning his legs while he was in the wheelchair, putting a book or papers on the tray of his wheelchair in a particular place, and opening the satchel on the back of his wheelchair to put something in or take something out for him. At some point after I was working at the hospital, it was necessary for Father to have an alarm placed on the satchel on the back of his wheelchair to alert him when it was being opened. There were times before when money was taken from the satchel while he was sitting in the wheelchair. He couldn't turn around to see who was behind him and sometimes a group of people talked to him as a distraction while someone else stole money from his satchel. The money he kept there belonged to the Chapel Fund and it didn't belong to him. It was money to be used for operating the chapel.

Father Kram was always learning new things. He was a whiz on the computer and he learned new practices as they developed. I remember once he took a memory course that taught one to put things in different rooms in one's mind in order to improve the memory. We all take for granted that we have the ability to make notes and write in planners and use our iPads, but Father couldn't do that and he had to commit things to memory as they occurred until he could have someone write them down or he could get back to his typewriter or computer to record them. He taught me that one is never too old to learn new things. He was very open-minded about progress and new inventions. In fact, he was an inventor himself.

Father Kram was the one person to whom I could go with my questions on many subjects—my spiritual advisor of sorts, though at that time of my life, I was busy with work and then later raising my daughter with my husband's help, and just being caught up in life in general. My husband and I had our one and only child after nine years of marriage. I talked to Father a lot about our desire to have a child and asked his advice on the various treatments available to us. I remember specifically that, at that time, in vitro fertilization became a popular procedure. In one discussion with Father, I reasoned with him that we so very badly desired a child of our own that it couldn't possibly be a bad way to achieve it. Father Kram advised me that to create a child through such a method would be wrong even though the outcome would be good. Sort of like two wrongs don't make a right. It really wasn't what I wanted to hear, but he was right. So we did what we could until the doctors in Houston told my husband and me that the best route to having a child would be adoption because problems with my reproductive organs made it impossible for me to become pregnant. After a period of grieving, we began the adoption process. It was discouraging because of the cost and the length of the process. In the meantime, we continued to pray for a child, whether our own or through adoption. In January 1991, right before my husband was to leave for Desert Storm, I discovered that I was pregnant. My husband did not deploy at that time and everything went well and we were blessed with our miracle baby in September 1991. She is now twenty-two years old. Father

Kram was very happy for us when Jenna was born and he told me her patron saint was St. Gemma. We gave her the name Marie as her middle name in honor of Mary, the Blessed Mother of God.

Karen Roznovsky's reflection is a long one, but it contains a glimpse of Fr. Kram's hospital ministry that is important to his story, and so we will continue with it.

The one thing that I always thought about was how dependent Father was on his caretakers. He had to totally trust them and sometimes there were caretakers who were so busy with the patients, they temporarily overlooked attending to his needs. That must have tested the very core of his faith. Really, his only choice was to put it in God's hands: "Thy Will Be Done." Father's way of dealing with difficult situations was not to complain and to be as cooperative as possible. He must have been very tired and uncomfortable at times from being in his wheelchair all day, but he had no choice except to wait. And then, there were times, when the nurses couldn't help him out of bed until much later in the morning. Again, he had no choice but to wait. Truly he was a man with the patience of Job.

I could tell that some people would avoid Father at first because they didn't seem to know how to approach him. He was insecure about how he had to breathe, that is the use of "frog breathing," and once asked if it was distracting. There were people who would actually ask him why he did that. I assured him that it was not distracting. Most people, though, especially the children, didn't even seem to notice and just saw him as a person and accepted his handicap as it was. Children are naturally curious and, after all, Father was sitting in a chair that rolled and slept in a bed that rocked.

Father Kram always supplied the hospital with items that he paid for like writing pads and pencils for the patients' rooms, mugs, caps, letter openers, and the like. He was always coming up with new public relation promotion items for which he provided the funds.

He concerned himself about the state of the hospital through the years when we didn't know if it would survive financially. I sincerely believe that Fr. Kram prayed the hospital through all those bad times and that he is still with us today. I attribute survival of the hospital and the ability to continue to serve the patients of Yoakum and the surrounding area to Father's continued prayers, as he looks over us. Besides wondering what would become of his "home" if the hospital were to close, he was concerned about the needs of the patients and the hospital employees who needed the hospital in Yoakum.

(In speaking of the hospital, we need to remember that this story began in the old hospital at 303 Hubbard Street and ends at the new hospital at 1200 Carl Ramert Drive, both in Yoakum.)
Karen Roznovsky continues her story.

I loved the chapel in the old hospital. The one in the new hospital is okay, but it never did quite feel like home. I attended daily Mass as often as I could at 4 p.m. at the old location. Since the Mass was always only about a half hour, I was rarely missed at work and my office was nearby in case I was needed. I don't recall any employee being discouraged from attending Mass. A small group of employees and several neighborhood residents comprised the daily congregation. On Sundays, though, it was always an overflow crowd with some attendees having to stand outside the chapel in the hall. Father's celebration of the Mass was such a joyous occasion that many people preferred his Mass in the chapel to one in the large and beautiful church down the street. His homilies were always short but interesting and applicable. Everyone usually came away with the feeling that whatever his topic was, Fr. Kram was personally addressing their own situation. It seemed that what he had to say really impacted our lives. It was like he was talking directly to each of us as individuals. I often had the privilege to assist him as Lector doing one of the readings in the Liturgy of the Word.

To this day, I miss him as a priest, as a confidant, as a friend. He was truly "One of a Kind." I love you, Fr. Kram.

Karen's sister, Janet Fikac Pohl, gives us another glimpse of Fr. Charles's hospital ministry in her reflection on his life. Here is what she wrote:

My earliest memories of Fr. Charles Kram were from grade school. I remember our class making a visit to see him and his parents. I don't remember why the bus couldn't make it up the drive to the house, but we walked a short distance kind of uphill. We sang Christmas carols for the Kram family and gave them a bag of oranges as a gift. The Krams were elderly but they still managed to take care of their son. I remember seeing his wheelchair and his bed that rocked back and forth to assist him in his breathing. The Krams were quiet but friendly and smiling and they were most willing to share their story with us. I also remember that when Fr. Kram was going to be ordained as a priest in our parish, Sts. Cyril and Methodius Catholic Church, our class was discussing who was going to attend. I remember really wanting to attend, but we lived out on a farm and, back then, people didn't drive to town at the drop of a hat like we do now. I do, however, remember watching his ordination on the news on television. It was awesome to see Fr. Kram being ordained in our small hometown church on the news and after so many years after being stricken by polio.

Who would have known that years later our paths would cross again? I began employment at Huth Memorial Hospital in 1982. I remember seeing Father around the hospital, but our paths didn't always cross in the beginning. I remember the annual "surprise" birthday parties because I often baked his cake and his favorite was German Chocolate. In

1987, I enrolled in the LVN Nursing Program at Huth Memorial Hospital and that's when I really began to know Father. Sister Paschaline Kutac was our instructor and everything was "a learning experience." Every student got a chance to take care of Father. His unique challenges were indeed learning experiences. Once he even allowed us to lie in his bed and experience the rocking motion. I remember feeling a little anxious at first (not knowing if I would slip out of the top or not). But, once I got used to it, it really wasn't so scary. After nursing school, I continued to work at the hospital as an LVN and I had several more opportunities to assist with Father's daily needs—from bathing him in bed to feeding him breakfast in bed. Then we dressed him for the day. That was a real workout since he was unable to help in any way, being paralyzed as he was. We had to roll him from side to side to put his clothes on him. After that, three or four nurses and nurse aides would physically lift him (one holding his head, another his shoulders, one his bottom, and one his legs). We would, as gently as possible, place him into his wheelchair where he spent his day until he would be put back into bed in the evening. Once Father was up and in his wheelchair, there was no stopping him. He required little assistance but when he did need help, he was always patient while awaiting help. Father was able to go just about anywhere in the hospital, even in the old hospital that was three stories high. He would go up and down the elevator by himself and he used a special stick in his mouth to press the elevator buttons. He also liked to sit just outside the front door of the hospital and he would greet the many people coming in and going out of the building.

Father usually ate lunch and dinner while sitting in his wheelchair. He had a plate with a brace on one end (sort of a backstop). We would get his food arranged, cut up, seasoned, and then he would eat on his own with a spoon that was attached to a syringe barrel that fit onto his fingers.

With the pivot of the sling that held his arm up, he would feed himself.

Father was famous for his little hideouts. If he got hungry for a candy bar or something, he knew where everything was and he would ask someone to retrieve it for him. He was generous with his hoard, always offering some to us. Father enjoyed eating unique foods. I remember someone making pig-in-the-blanket treats for him with mustard and onions. He also liked sardines and head sausage.

Getting Father back into bed required at least three people. Sometimes when Dr. Ciborowski was around, he would lift Father into bed with the assistance of the charge nurse to help him and they would prepare Father for the night. We would lift Father as gently as possible from his wheelchair back into his waiting bed. Once he was settled back into bed, we would move his legs slightly back and forth until he told us he was comfortable. We did this because he couldn't move them later if he was uncomfortable. His respirator was hooked to his trachea with the tubing lying by his side and also adjusted until he was comfortable. Sometimes we would even have to adjust the settings on the respirator. Father would tell us what setting he desired for the machine. We would then put the string for his call bell system and TV access (a box that he invented and had someone make for him) into his mouth so he would be able to call for assistance or to watch TV whenever he chose. Once in bed, Father usually didn't require much help. Sometimes he got the "munchies" and we would feed him from his stash of food. Sometimes he would ask us to adjust his feet or the tubing so he would be more comfortable. And sometimes he would have an itch, usually on his nose or on the top of his head, and he would ask us to rub the areas with a dry washcloth until he was comfortable again. I did not work the night shift (10 p.m. to 6 a.m.), but at some point in the night, Fr. Kram would be taken off the respirator and his bed would be turned on to rock back and forth. He would also call the nurses when he felt the urge to move his bowels and he would be put on a bedpan. Day in and day out, it was the same routine. In all this, Father was always patient and he waited until help arrived. He never complained or demanded help immediately.

As time went on, I moved from nursing to working in the nursing administration office and I saw Father's ministry from another point of view. Sometimes I had a little extra time and I would help him with little things like opening his mail and writing checks. I would place a small homemade brace that fit on his hand that had a clothespin attached, place a pen in it, line up the checkbook in exactly the right place for him (remember that his hand movement was limited by a special brace attached to his wheelchair) and he would write a check. His handwriting was a little shaky, but it was always legible. Sometimes I would help him get ready to anoint someone. I would place all of the items he would need on his tray along with the prayer cards he used. With that set-up, he would go on his appointed rounds to see the patients.

When Father was working on his homilies, he needed help removing the written work from the printer and filing them in the proper folders. Everything was well organized and he knew exactly where everything was (or was supposed to be). He spent a lot of time on his computer writing or revising his homilies and other writings. It always amazed me to see him working at his computer with his stick in his mouth and punching the keys that way. He was even faster than I was on the computer in those early years when I was learning to use a computer.

It was also amazing to see how many lives he touched. The mail he received surprised me. He always loved Christmas and I still miss him today, especially around Christmas time. He received so many cards from people wanting prayers or just those who wrote to wish him well. There was a special lady who wrote him often. Her nickname was "Yellow Rose." I think I enjoyed her letters and cards as much as he did. She mostly asked for prayers or thanked him for prayers for herself or family and friends. I set up a nativity scene in the chapel every year. I continue to do so and it brings back so many fond memories of him. It is an honor to display it as he would want it done if he was still here.

Father was always there for the patients and he never met a stranger. A person's religious background didn't matter to him. Everyone loved him. He touched so many lives in so many ways. He wasn't wealthy but he shared what he did have with those in need. He helped many people financially when they were in need. He also liked supporting local charities and bought raffle tickets for every event in the area. He always said that if he won a prize (which he never did, as far as I know), he would give the prize away since he never needed any of "that stuff" anyway.

In July 1997, we moved to the new hospital. A lot of things changed with that move. I sometimes wonder if this move was the beginning of the final chapter in his life. The Sisters were no longer with the hospital and other changes were happening. The new hospital was beautiful, but not as easily accessible to Father. There were closed doors everywhere (patient privacy had become a big issue). Father could not open the doors. He would patiently wait outside doors for someone to assist him. His familiar and comfortable home for so many years in the old hospital was gone, but he made the best he could of his circumstances. Father had a new room that had to be set up and he continued with his organized ways of doing things. I helped him as much as I could. His handwriting was more illegible than ever and he added me to his bank account as a signatory so I could write his checks. A lot of personnel changes took place and many new people had new levels of work load and really didn't have the time or patience to assist him as before.

Father Kram asked very little of others and when he did, it was always "when you have time." He never demanded anything, especially the care he received upon which he was totally dependent upon the staff. He was patient and never complained, even when people grew impatient with him.

I will forever miss his Masses. They were inspirational and ended with a joke he had heard somewhere. The sound of his wheelchair is no longer heard coming down the hallway or around the corner. He is no longer with us in body, but will always remain in our hearts. When I pass by his picture in the hall just outside the chapel, I can still feel the love in his eyes as though he is still watching over us. I still talk to him when things get tough and I need a little "pick me up." Father was my rock and still is when I think I can't cope or deal with things in my life. At times like these, I remember how strong he was and that he never complained and that's what helps get me through life's many challenges to this very day.

What a beautiful reflection that is!

One of Fr. Charles's cousins, Lanelle Sommerlatte Kasper, was nearly his same age. They grew up as neighbors and classmates at Bunjes School and shared many memories over the years about their childhood pastimes. Later in life as she recalled his hospital ministry, she admired his ability to inspire people to be their best, to make the best of their present circumstances. When her husband suffered a stroke, he was confined to the hospital for an extended period. Father Charles made it a point to visit him in his room every evening and to share memories with him and Lanelle. Then in 1995, Lanelle suffered a stroke and she was a patient in the hospital. Father Charles helped her recover the use of her arms and legs through his inspiring encouragement to keep trying, to keep trying to do her best.

Again we see the attitude: *Make the best you can of your present circumstances.*

Another cousin, Elton Zander, and his wife Lillie, recalled how Fr. Charles once told them there was only one patient who refused to let Father visit her again. He said the doctor told him that the woman was so absorbed in herself that she couldn't see anything or anyone else in the world. Elton and Lillie agreed that Fr. Charles was such a joy to be around that they couldn't understand any negative reaction to his presence. They commented that once Fr. Charles mentioned his life was certainly different from what he had expected it to be and that God obviously had plans for him he hadn't imagined. Lillie recalled telling him, "You have reached more lives in a Christian way in the hospital and you have touched more lives in your condition than you could have if you had not become an invalid. You would have been ministering in the Catholic Church and serving God well, but all the other denominations would not have had the blessings of having you in their lives." By the way, Elton and Lillie worshipped in the Methodist Church.

A close friend, Phyllis Lauer, offered these thoughts about Fr. Charles's ministry:

> Father Kram was a very good listener and he had a wonderful sense of humor. He was patient and kind. He focused on others and not himself and he had a way of making you feel important or special. He was open and approachable. He was able to put himself "in your shoes." He readily understood your pain, worries, cares, pleasures, joys, and suffering. I admired very much his fortitude. Maybe it was his physical handicap that made me most aware of this virtue. He had such a strong will to do good in all things despite his physical limitations. He didn't see himself with pity. He felt very blessed. By his bearing, he gave dignity to everyone around him. So many times, he was in pain but he offered his suffering to Christ. He knew God would give

him the sanctifying grace to sustain him. You always felt uplifted in his presence.

Over the years, he sat by so many patients' beds comforting the sick and the dying. Being sick puts many people in a position of being scared, sometimes angry, even worried at times. Patients' emotions can surface in many directions. Father Kram had that unique way of disarming the negative feelings by gently listening and patiently showing genuine Christian love and understanding. I think people readily felt that he understood pain and anxiety and theirs melted away under his loving manners. I truly believe that Fr. Kram was the holiest and most Christ-like person I have ever met. I sure miss his presence. Being around him made me feel holy.

Another friend, Emma Raska, who knew him for the last twenty-two years of his life offered these recollections: "He was my dear friend and counselor. He was a man of enormous faith and he never questioned why God had allowed his infirmities. He trusted God in all matters. In fact, he gloried in his infirmities. He felt that they were his share of Christ's suffering and he meant to bear his share with dignity."

It is appropriate that we turn to Fr. Charles for some comments of his own about his hospital ministry. Here are some comments he sent to the seminarians in San Antonio:

I have not found my hospital ministry to be at all depressing. I get around in a powered wheelchair and use a long mouth-stick to punch the elevator buttons that make it possible for me to go to all three floors. Mike, the maintenance chief, calls me the "hot rod priest." I make rounds every day and visit patients of all faiths. My patients' list gives name, room number, and religion, so it is easy to get acquainted and offer love and moral support and prayers. Once in a while some able-bodied person will say, "Oh, if only you were healed, think of how then you could really do the Lord's work." Actually, I consider my physical condition to be an asset. People are very helpful and considerate. For example, when a patient needs anointing of the sick, it is easy to find someone to help get out the Prayers and oil and put on my stole and lower the bed rails. In the hospital, the sacraments do indeed become truly meaningful and consoling. I am not able to distribute Holy Communion, but in the evening I always leave a list of the next morning's communicants at the Chapel door for a special minister, who helps me drive up a ramp to the altar and does whatever needs to be done to make the Mass go smoothly. On Sunday, generally about thirty people are in attendance, at which time I preach. As for my social life, I hardly ever go anywhere, but as Hospital Chaplain, I meet such a variety of people that I certainly do not feel deprived or isolated. I enjoy giving people a tour of my room which features a number of self-help inventions and a bed that rocks like a see-saw, as an aid to respiration.

Today pastoral care is a profession with many techniques. For me, it is a ministry of strength and consolation to the sick and their loved ones, and of reassurance that in spite of isolation in a hospital, the bonds of love and grace remain unbroken. I conclude that the essence of pastoral care is understanding, caring, and often just being there.

Father Charles wisely added, "The true calling of the Hospital Chaplain is the Pastoral care of the sick. Indeed, the Lord has said that the poor would always be with us; so will the sick and the weak and the aged and the dying. My greatest consolation is to know with ever greater certainty that I belong to them."

At one time, Fr. Charles was asked to share a few thoughts with the hospital staff and patients about his hospital chaplaincy. Here are some of those thoughts:

I am gadget-oriented and use mouth sticks for almost everything. In fact, since early 1986, I have been using a computer, modified for mouth stick operation, to do word processing and spreadsheets. I also take great pride in being in charge of hospital souvenirs—caps, mugs, letter openers, T-shirts, pill containers, writing pads, pencils and balloons for the kids.

The local fire department has made me their chaplain, which gives me many chances to eat oysters and barbecue and maintain good relations with the fire fighters and ambulance drivers.

I administer the Chapel Fund, which enables me to assist the indigent by paying for such things as canes, walkers, baby car seats, diapers, prescription drugs, and, to some extent, rent, food, and utilities. As a member of the local Ministerial Alliance, I especially appreciate the many opportunities to promote mutual goodwill and confidence among the church-goers in our area.

The Most Reverend Charles V. Grahmann, Bishop Emeritus of Dallas, made these observations in 2009 when he reflected on his association with Fr. Charles:

In 1982 the new Diocese of Victoria was established by Pope John Paul II. I was assigned as the first bishop of this new diocese. Since Fr. Kram now became one of my priests of the new diocese, I chose to visit him regularly at the hospital in Yoakum.

On one occasion, I was invited to attend a meeting of the administration of the hospital and the doctors on the Board of Directors. They wished to give me an update on the presence of Fr. Charles Kram in the hospital. One of the doctors said: "He does more healing than we do with all of our medical skills. Every day he rolls around visiting all the people, giving them hope we can't give."

When I left that meeting, I finally realized that indeed it was all worth it. The suggestion of Msgr. Alois Goertz, the concurrence of Msgr. Thomas Lyssy, Fathers John Yanta and Larry Stuebben, indeed was a gift of the Holy Spirit. I don't think we realized the depth of what we were asking.

Many holy people were a part of this great drama of a humble man, afflicted with polio, his beloved parents who cared for him, and what God had in store for them. I am happy to have been a small part of this miracle.

An example of the spiritual healing that God worked through this remarkable servant of his is found in this story from Marjorie Welfl Knebel of Weimar, Texas. She wrote:

In 1957 my family moved from Moulton to Shiner. I was ten years old and attended St. Ludmila's Academy in Shiner. Within a year or two there, I joined a young girl's Catholic group called Junior Catholic Daughters. To the best of my recollection Mrs. Marie Wagner was our director/sponsor. She arranged for us to visit Charles Kram, who, at the time, was a young man living with his family in the countryside of Shiner. Charles had a very unique and extraordinary hobby; he was a short wave radio operator. He had a set-up that would be the envy of any young man in Lavaca County. We were certainly more interested in the fact that he could call people all over the United States than his being quadriplegic and in a wheelchair. Our little group knew even then that this man was exceptional, but we did not feel that he was necessarily a holy man. He was just warm and friendly, and we were eager to learn what he was doing with that short wave radio.

I moved away from Shiner in 1966 and made my home in Houston and later in Katy. It wasn't until 1992, during the illness of my mother (at that time age eighty-two) that I was reacquainted with Charles Kram, who was now a priest residing at Huth Memorial Hospital in Yoakum. What a wonderful opportunity to see him again. I didn't immediately realize it was the same person. Mother was a very private person and Fr. Kram wanted to visit her, but we knew mother would be reluctant to see anyone. Mother was in very poor condition—physically, emotionally, and psychologically. But upon his encouragement, we agreed to let him come to see her to perform the prayer for the sick. My sister, Marilyn, and I were very hesitant about doing this because mother was incoherent and uncontrollable. To be perfectly honest, we were at our wits end with mother and her emotional state.

That evening, Fr. Kram came into her room and brought the holy oils with him to anoint her. I told Father that if he had a double dose to please use it because mother needed all the help she could possibly get from the Lord. My sister and I assisted him and he prayed for her comfort and then anointed her. He spoke a few words to us and left the room.

I have been very fortunate in my life to feel the presence of the Holy Spirit surround me on several occasions and that evening his spirit filled the room with love and mother was blessed. No longer did she rant and rave, but was quiet and at peace. Father Kram made this happen. It was a miracle.

Mother lived another four and a half years in complete peace in the Shiner nursing home.

Harvey Stary of Cuero tells the story of when he and his first wife lived in Yoakum. She became ill and died. Harvey was struck a tremendous blow by her passing. Not long after her death, Harvey was visiting a friend who was a patient in the hospital and he met Fr. Charles. They spent many hours together in prayer and conversation. He says he wouldn't have survived that loss if it hadn't been for the gentle consoling spiritual guidance of Fr. Charles. During this experience, they became such good friends that when Father died, Harvey served as one of his pallbearers. Tears still swell in Harvey's eyes when he recalls the tender loving guidance he received from him.

It's interesting to note that another Cuero resident remembers Fr. Kram from when she and her family lived in Yoakum. Kathy Morrow says when she and her husband, Bill, had small children (they had three daughters), they often went to the Sunday 11:30 a.m. Mass at the hospital. They were drawn there by the way Fr. Charles celebrated Mass. On one particular occasion, one of the girls was being restless and noisy during Father's homily. Kathy got up to take the child out of the chapel and Father, in the middle of his homily, told Kathy, "Don't take her out of church; she is just praying to God in a child's way. Please stay." Kathy smiles as she recalls his gentle loving way of easing a parent's embarrassment over an overactive child. "What compassion he had," she said.

Sister Elaine Braden, IWBS, recalls that Fr. Charles was long-suffering without complaints, patient, always in good spirits, kind, gentle, and humorous. She served at St. Ludmila and knew him for at least twenty-five years. They shared an enormous love of God and neighbor, and she often assisted him in the celebration of the Mass. She beams with joy as she recalls pouring the wine and water into the chalice and elevating the Sacred Host and the Chalice of Precious Blood as Father's hands during the Most Sacred Consecration when the Holy Spirit transformed the bread and wine into the Body and Blood of Christ. That was an awesome moment in her day and she still cherishes the memory.

She sang his praises for the loving manner in which he visited the patients in their rooms, consoled them in their anxieties, administered the sacraments, and always raised the spirits of the patients despite his own pain and suffering.

When you ask John Butschek of Hallettsville about Fr. Charles, you set in motion an avalanche of admiration. John gave these thoughts and recollections:

> In September of 1946, I started my fifth year at St. John's Seminary in San Antonio, Texas. Charles Kram, who had just graduated from Shiner Catholic High School in May of 1946, entered St. John's and we were classmates until October, when I left the seminary and continued my life in the secular world and Charles continued his at the seminary. I knew very little of his life except that I had heard he had contracted polio.
>
> When I retired in 1990, I decided to renew my acquaintance. Entering Father's room in the Yoakum hospital, I found Father in an antique wheel chair. He looked up and

without any hesitation said, "Johnny Butschek!" Forty-four years had passed since I had seen him and I could hardly believe how much he knew about my life. Each visit, after that, led to another.

When I offered to help him in any way he wanted, he said, "If you will grease all the fittings, tighten the drive belts, etc. on my chair, I would appreciate it." That chair did indeed need attention. It was a standard manual chair that had been converted to electric drive with custom-made controls so he could control the movement by a perpendicular stem in front that was anchored to a tray on his chair. On top of the iron stem was a soft ball that he could move with his chin. This gave him control of the chair via electric motors on the wheels.

As the visits continued and our friendship grew, Father became more at ease asking me to do more things. His first and foremost concern, however, was not to be a bother to anyone.

Father had many small tools and it was easy to see that before he was stricken with polio, he must have enjoyed working with his hands. His chair required mechanical and electrical equipment of ages gone by to keep it working. One reason he liked the old chair was his complete knowledge of all the parts. When I would work on things, insofar as possible, I would always work in front where he could see and direct me. He would direct me in all things. I was his hands. He would constantly apologize for giving me so many instructions and would ask, "Does this offend you when I always tell you what to do?" I am not known for my patience, but with him, it truly was a pleasure to see the enjoyment he got.

On one occasion, when we were visiting, some beads of perspiration formed on his forehead. One slipped into his eye and began to irritate him, so he asked me to wipe the sweat away. Imagine having to ask someone to wipe a drop of sweat from your eye. He was so helpless! So dependent!

At times Father would develop phlegm in his throat. With his permanent tracheotomy and weakened lungs, he needed help to dislodge the phlegm. The nurses would attach a suction machine to the trachea. The machine was manually adjusted to give the correct suction. A setting too high or too low would cause problems. Once when I was with Father, he had the machine on but it needed adjustment. He rang for a nurse, but none came. Between gasping for air and choking, he instructed me to adjust it. Time was critical until I hit the right setting. I was anxious. He must have been frantic, but he didn't show it.

Another thing that impressed me greatly were his shelves of personal things—tools, supplies of varied kinds, papers, etc. He knew what each box contained, and where it belonged on the shelves. Each box was numbered, and while we were working, he would direct me by shelf and box number for whatever we needed. These are some of the things I mention about the man. Father Kram, the priest, is even more impressive. Totally paralyzed from the neck down, with the assistance of a second person, he would say Mass, deliver sermons, and edify anyone who could imagine him as an *alter Christus*. One couldn't help but think of the silent sufferings of Christ carrying his cross to Calvary, being crucified, and praying for his crucifiers! This priest seemed to offer himself in a similar fashion. In the months and years we visited, I never, not once, heard him complain or seem depressed about his state of life. In fact, in his chair, he was always visiting, consoling, preaching (sometimes without saying a word), and uplifting his flock. It was common to hear people say, "How can I, or anyone, complain after a visit with Fr. Kram?"

When he left this world in August 2000, there is no question in my mind the Lord received him with open arms.

I no longer have the pleasure of his mortal visits, but we communicate frequently. I have one regret: I could have, should have, done more for Father. He certainly did much for me. He still does. What a friend I have!

Deacon Linard Harper and his wife, Dot, recall how Fr. Charles could relate to people in pain due to his own experiences and he could ease the burden of pain in the patients with his gentle, loving manner. They also recall that he performed a number of baptisms and marriages in the hospital chapel. He frequently heard people's confessions as he administered the sacrament of reconciliation. Word of his kind and loving understanding in the act of administering God's forgiveness brought him many people including priests and nuns for this beautiful gift of love.

God truly chose the right person for this ministry.

What a remarkable man!

Here are a few thoughts of his on dealing with someone's death:

When someone has died, we all want to say the right thing, so we quote a Scripture verse or say, "It's God's Will" or something like that, but that doesn't work. The survivors don't want their loved one dead.

The kindest words I heard at my dad's funeral were from an old seminary buddy, who waved and said, "Hi, Charlie." When someone dies here in the emergency room or in their room, I just say, "I offer you my love and moral support."

Try it sometime if you don't know what to say.

In 1994, the Hospital Board was developing plans for a new hospital. Rumors were flying about just about every subject that people could bring up. One such subject was: "What is going to happen to Fr. Kram?"

The Yoakum Hospital District Board passed the following resolution:

RESOLUTION NO. 59

WHEREAS, Reverend Charles Kram has resided in the Yoakum Community Hospital since February 1977.

WHEREAS, Reverend Charles Kram has made an invaluable contribution to the Hospital and its patients through his Pastoral Care Program.

WHEREAS, Reverend Charles Kram is an integral part of Yoakum Community Hospital and provides the "perfect economy" in terms of his needs and that of the Hospital being in harmony.

WHEREAS, regardless of religious conviction or church affiliation, people, in this community, are unified in wanting Reverend Kram to be assured of residence and purpose in the replacement hospital.

THEREFORE, BE IT RESOLVED that the Hospital District Board, recognizing the past contributions of Reverend Kram, desires that Reverend Kram will continue to enjoy space and purpose in the successor facility for the indefinite future.

ADOPTED this 14th day of July, 1994

Yoakum Hospital District

(signed) Jim Witte, President

ATTEST:

Bert C. West, Secretary

That put to rest that matter.

Probably the best commentary about Fr. Kram's hospital ministry really comes from him himself. Here are some of his thoughts on that subject:

> It is surprising how much one can do, given appropriate equipment and a supporting hand. I make rounds in a powered wheelchair. My patients' list gives name, room number, and religion. My technique is to bump the door open, call the patient by name, and ask, "Do you feel like a visitor today?" Then I drive up close to the bed and converse and offer a prayer. No one refuses a prayer and the common bond that soon develops is truly touching. A patient will run through his list of ailments and then say something like, "I know you understand; you've been there." The tone for my ministry is set and all I have to do is dispense God's love. The joy of this service is without equal.

CHAPTER NINE

In Sickness and in Health

Beloved, do not be surprised that a trial by fire is occurring among you, as if
something strange were happening to you. But rejoice to the extent that you
share in the sufferings of Christ, so that when his glory is revealed, you may
also rejoice exultantly. (1 Peter 4:12–13)

We have seen earlier in this story how Charles Kram, Jr., grew
up on a farm two miles east of Shiner, Texas, doing all the
activities of a healthy child and then of a growing boy and finally
of a teenager who entered St. John's Seminary in San Antonio to
study and prepare himself for service to God as a Catholic priest.
We have seen how, in the peak of good health, at the age of twenty-
three, he was cruelly stricken with the crippling effects of polio, a
disease that turned him into a quadriplegic, totally dependent on
caregivers to provide for him the most basic hygienic necessities of
life.

In Chapter Four, we saw how his elderly parents cared for him
in their home on the farm for twenty-five years. Suddenly he found
himself homeless (or shall we say, without caregivers) in the winter
of 1977 when his father died and his mother was confined to a
nursing home suffering the effects of a major stroke.

We saw how God provided a solution to Fr. Charles's need for
caregivers when Archbishop Furey of San Antonio assigned him to
Huth Memorial Hospital in Yoakum as hospital chaplain.

Mary Butschek observed: "In my opinion, Fr. Kram was the
personification of humility and patience. He had absolutely no

privacy. He was totally at the mercy of others to see about taking care of his bodily needs, yet he accepted his situation with courage and dignity. He was very appreciative of even the smallest kindness shown to him."

Hazel Pfeil was Fr. Charles's age and served as one of his nurses for over twenty years. She gave us this recollection of what Mary Butschek meant:

> About 4 a.m., he would wake from sleep with the rocking bed on all night. He was then connected to a respirator to help with his breathing. This was connected to his tracheotomy tube that was installed during a severe bout with pneumonia. His chest muscles were so weak he had difficulty coughing. The trachea opening was made permanent to facilitate the removal of phlegm from his lungs. This removal is done with a suction device that operates somewhat like a vacuum that draws the mucus out of the lungs. This procedure is necessary to prevent infection from occurring in the lungs. He was so prone to lung infections that the suction procedure was a frequent occurrence every day.

> He was bathed completely by a nurse who also applied lotion to his entire body. He was then fitted with a corset to help his back and elastic anti-embolic stockings to prevent swelling in his legs and feet. He was then dressed in his cleric clothes and placed in his wheelchair. Most of these maneuvers required several persons because he was unable to do anything for himself. To put him in the wheelchair, they connected him to a sling that was used as a "lifter" to raise him off the bed and onto the wheelchair.

> He remained in the wheelchair until it was time for him to be put to bed when the entire process was performed in reverse order.

Hazel also recalled that for Father to call a nurse to come to his aid when he was in bed, he had to use a procedure he devised whereby he kept in his mouth a string that was attached to the nurse's call system. To trigger the call system, he shortened the string in his mouth with movement of his tongue and lips until the call alert was activated. This was not a small achievement as it required much effort on his part. But remember, he was totally helpless, totally dependent on other people to do the normal things in life that we do unconsciously.

Mrs. Pfeil added these personal comments: "If he ever felt 'down' over his situation, you would never know it because he never complained about anything. He was always so very appreciative of everything that was done for him and he was always so 'upbeat'. I always wished I could do more for him. He was truly a wonderful man of God and we all loved him very much."

Another nurse, Jan Roberts, offered these interesting thoughts on Fr. Kram's life:

I often told Fr. Kram that he could type faster with the stick in his mouth than I could with ten fingers.

The children who saw Father sitting in his wheelchair with the splints on his hands and the stick in his mouth were so intrigued. He cheerfully told them about having polio and why he had to use the devices he had.

Father enjoyed going out of the hospital (especially to gatherings such as picnics), but he wanted to go only if one of the nurses who could operate the suction device could accompany him.

Jan continued her story:

Julia Moreno, who worked as a nurse's aide at the hospital, was very protective of Father. She would get so upset if she felt another staff member didn't give the tender loving care to him that she always gave.

Father was such a generous person. He often wrote checks to people in need so they could pay for groceries, utility bills, etc. He was usually much more concerned about others than about himself.

Dr. Ciborowski checked on Father every day and listened to his lungs so he could notice any changes in an effort to keep ahead of potential lung problems.

Father had a great sense of humor. He often told us jokes and stories that were amusing.

I felt privileged to go to Mass when Father was celebrating the Liturgy, especially when I could assist him. Father was delighted when one of the nurses asked him to officiate at her wedding. He said he would be comfortable doing it since I would be able to bring him to the wedding and be available to clear his lungs if the need would arise.

He taught me so much about patience. I know it would be difficult for me to depend on everyone as he did for so many things.

When I first was introduced to Father, he was lying on his rocking bed. I thought, "How cool!" I soon found out what a necessity it was for him. Many children thought how neat it would be to sleep on a bed like that. In fact, Father let some of us try it out to see how it felt. It wasn't as cool as we thought it would be.

Father Kram was a therapist of sorts. He often spoke to patients and families who were upset or depressed. He was such an inspiration to so many. He was also always available to give the Sacrament of the Sick to the sick and dying.

Joseph Jakubik was a friend for many years. He offered these thoughts about Fr. Kram:

I first met Fr. Kram when I entered high school at St. John's Seminary in San Antonio in 1948. There was limited contact allowed between minor seminarians like me and major seminarians like Charles Kram, but since we were from neighboring parishes back home, we did manage to visit on occasion. I had just finished high school (minor seminary) when he was stricken with polio. I saw him very rarely when he was with his parents on the farm near Shiner.

In 1956 I left the seminary and went about my life as a layman. My mother lived only a block away from the Huth Memorial Hospital and when I visited her, we would go to Mass at the hospital after Father became the chaplain there. I was able to renew my acquaintance with him. In 1988 I moved into my mother's home and often attended Mass at the hospital. It was my pleasure to assist Fr. Charles in his ministry and I was honored that he had requested that I be one of his pallbearers at his funeral.

In all the time I was associated with him, I never heard him complain about his affliction or find fault with anyone. There was always joy about him and he had an uplifting effect on everyone around him. He had that unique ability to turn a negative into a positive. For example, he was totally dependent on others to do for him all the things he could not do for himself. Instead of this being a burden on everyone, it became their pleasure to help him. His tremendous courage and faith in God and his fellow human beings stimulated those around him to try to be more like him.

Sister Paschaline Kutac, IWBS, was one of the many people who shared their thoughts and memories of Fr. Kram with us as we gathered information about his life. Here are some of her thoughts:

I had the privilege of knowing Fr. Kram for sixteen years while I was in Yoakum. One of my greatest privileges was to assist him with the Mass. Father would pray the Mass very reverently, even on the days when he was really, really sick. Sometimes during the prayers, he would become very ill and would need to be suctioned. There was nothing to do but take him to his room and attach him to the suction machine and clear the phlegm from his lungs. Then we would return to the chapel to continue with the Mass. The people understood what was happening and they remained in the chapel during his absence, usually praying for his welfare.

Sister added these comments:

Another thing I remember about him is how charitable he was. People would come to him and ask for help. I remember a particularly sad situation where a person needing money came to him because she didn't have enough money to buy food for her baby. He gave her the money without any questions asked. I kept after him to be sure these people really needed the money before he helped them. His attitude was that if they lied to him, they would have to answer to God for their faults. Eventually, he was suckered into giving someone money for gas for their car and they ended up spending it on booze. That's when he worked out a deal with a service station whereby they would give someone a certain amount of gas and charge it to Father with his written approval and he would then settle up with the station. Father was so honest and loving and innocent that he had a hard time believing that anyone could be a cheat and a liar and a thief.

It could truly be said that Father was the top layer of all that is good.

Those of us who did not know Fr. Kram personally might have a hard time understanding the many obstacles he and his caregivers had to overcome for his life to continue, but as we gather information from those who did know him and who worked around him, we marvel at his patience and endurance. And we who stand outside that circle of acquaintances must be in awe at the ingenuity of the medical profession and the Christ-like love with which his caregivers supported him, even in times of great sacrifice on their part. We are constantly reminded of the parable of the Good Samaritan. They treated him with mercy (Luke 10:29–37).

We turn now to the physician who cared for Fr. Kram in his later years for his observations. Crayton E. Ciborowski, M.D., offered these thoughts:

Father had a real bad bout of pneumonia and he wasn't my patient at that point, and Sister Mary Lela, who is now known as Anne Marie Germani, was Director of Nursing at that time and asked me to help him because his regular doctor was not available. His condition became an emergency when he suddenly stopped breathing. I took charge of his care at that moment. We did not have the facilities in Yoakum to handle his emergency, so we performed what measures we could and we moved him to Victoria. Unfortunately, there was no Pulmonary Specialist available when we arrived there so we had to quickly transfer him to San Antonio. We must have resembled a comedy act with Fr. Kram in the ambulance with the corresponding medical personnel attending to him followed by an eighteen-wheeler truck carrying his rocking bed plus several cars of medical personnel. Fortunately, we were able to arrange a police escort all the way to the hospital in San Antonio with siren and flashing red lights in full use. It was there that a tracheotomy was performed. This allowed him to breathe more freely.

He had restrictive and obstructive lung disease and because of this, he was quite susceptible to infection, and he couldn't clear his secretions very well. The recurring infections caused scar tissue to build up on his lungs. That condition added to his breathing problems. When you breathe, of course, before you get any fresh air into your lungs, you have to move all of the air in your sinuses, in your nose and your throat, down into your lungs before you get any benefit from the first little bit of fresh air. The tracheotomy, in his case, did two things. It avoided the dead space (of the nose and sinuses) and it enabled the nurses to clear the airways by suctioning out the secretions in his lungs. In this way, he got fewer infections and when he did, we were able to capture more directly a culture of the bacteria to determine the proper antibiotic to combat the infection.

The effects of the paralysis created a situation whereby Fr. Kram's life was much more fragile than one can imagine. Yet his spirits were always high and his enthusiasm for helping other people stimulated everyone around him to try to match his caring nature.

Dr. Crayton Ciborowski provided us with more information on Fr. Kram. For example, he comments that Fr. Kram was a very modest person and even after all the years of nurses and aides bathing him and caring for his personal hygienic needs, he was still embarrassed and bothered by these needs.

Toward the end of his life when it was discovered that Father had cancer on one of his kidneys, he revealed to Dr. Ciborowski that he was going to dedicate his suffering to the Lord.

In a most holy manner, Fr. Charles found peace and joy by sharing Christ's suffering on the cross through his own suffering. Christ did not complain or find fault with God or anyone else, and neither did Fr. Kram.

One of Father's long-time friends, Marjorie Rebecek Kresta, shared these thoughts with us:

> I first became acquainted with Fr. Charles in the late 1950s. I was a member of the Junior Catholic Daughters of the Americas and Fr. Charles was our pet charity. He was an inspiration to all of us. Despite his handicap, he was always willing to be of service to others.
>
> While serving as Chaplain at the local hospital, Fr. Charles never failed to visit each patient and offer prayers on their behalf, also anointing them with the holy oils if asked to do so. Father Charles, it seemed, never let his pain hinder him. He rolled from room to room in his wheelchair, visiting and praying with patients. He always had a kind word or maybe even a little joke to share with patients, family and friends.
>
> Father Charles touched me personally on many occasions, but one stands out in my mind. It was during my battle with breast cancer. One of my grandsons had just been born and I was at the hospital to see him. I ran into Fr. Charles, who was also fighting a personal battle with cancer. We

discussed our diseases for quite a while and then he said something that I will never forget. "Margie," he said, "in a thousand years, this won't matter at all."

Father Charles was so reverent, he was the perfect example of humility. He always seemed to be satisfied with whatever the Lord saw fit to send his way, including polio and the handicap that followed. Somehow, he found a way to use that for the honor and glory of God.

In 1985, Fr. Charles gave these thoughts to the readers of *Today's Catholic*, the official publication of the Archdiocese of San Antonio about his ministry as a hospital chaplain:

As the years go by, I find myself ever more in the shoes of those to whom I minister—with chronic ailments, recurring infections, and once, major surgery. But life has not been disappointing, considering that my life expectancy, which was only five years at the onset of my illness, has now stretched to thirty-three years, with almost ten years in the Priesthood. So, rather than waste time questioning God's Providence or wondering what will happen tomorrow, I keep moving on to the completion of my calling. I would say to everyone who reads this, let us keep each other in our prayers, and if you are ever in Yoakum, let me take you on a tour of the hospital.

Those are beautiful thoughts and we might think they were his finest, but look at what we found in one of his homilies:

Saint Teresa of Avila once knelt before the crucifix and asked Jesus, "Why do you let your friends suffer so much?" Jesus replied, "It is because I love them." The Saint answered, "No wonder you have so few friends."

She was right. We have a Savior who gained his victory by patient endurance. We know him by the nail prints in his hands and in his feet and by his wounded side. We must accept him, cross and all.

We aspire after greatness by always making love our first and finest motivation and by striving to be humble servants of all and the best that we can be.

Deacon Linard Harper knew Fr. Kram very well and he gave us these thoughts that are a fitting close for this chapter:

Father was a very positive individual. He loved to joke. He always had a joke to tell as he tried to uplift people. He often told people, "Don't look at me; look at yourselves. I'm only in this condition because God loves me. He loved me so much that he allowed me to do my suffering here on earth so I can get to heaven sooner."

That was basically his motto. God allowed me to have this kind of life so it would be my doorway to heaven.

Father was just a positive, loving person. I never heard a harsh word come out of his mouth. Many times he could have used harsh words when people mistreated him as some people did. I know of certain things that happened in the hospital that upset him but he didn't raise his voice and was not critical about what happened. He tried to work around the situation and keep all things peaceful. He loved being with the people and with peace among them all.

Make the best you can of your present circumstances.

CHAPTER TEN

Community Ministry

When the Son of Man comes in his glory, and all the angels with him, he will sit upon his glorious throne, and all the nations will be assembled before him. And he will separate them one from another, as a shepherd separates the sheep from the goats. He will place the sheep on his right and the goats on his left. Then the king will say to those on his right, "Come, you who are blessed by my Father. Inherit the kingdom prepared for you from the foundation of the world. For I was hungry and you gave me food, I was thirsty and you gave me drink, a stranger and you welcomed me, naked and you clothed me, ill and you cared for me, in prison and you visited me." Then the righteous will answer him and say, "Lord, when did we see you hungry and feed you, or thirsty and give you drink? When did we see you a stranger and welcome you, or naked and clothe you? When did we see you ill or in prison, and visit you?" And the king will say to them in reply, "Amen, I say to you whatever you did for one of these least brothers of mine, you did for me." (Matthew 25:31–40)

Father Charles often displayed and dispensed his wisdom for our benefit. Here are some wise and beautiful thoughts from him on Christian service:

The world is full of places and people dedicated to serving others.

There are service stations for our cars, hospitals and clinics for our health care, political institutions for public service, and many more. All of these require people willing to serve.

Where Jesus is concerned, his own special purpose was to serve. In the modern world, too, there are many opportunities for us, his followers, to serve.

When discussing Christian service, we tend to think mostly of the things we do in Church. Of course there are now many opportunities for the average Catholic to take a direct part in Church work, such as distributing Holy Communion, reading at Mass, teaching CCD, and such things as that, but we usually overlook the fact that many of the ordinary things we do every day can be made into a fine way of Christian service to others.

Suppose you are a child and your mother is tired after supper. Surprise her by leaving the TV and offering to clear the table and do the dishes. Why wait to be asked or told? You could consider doing favors for family members as your special home ministry. Or suppose a brother or sister or classmate of yours is doing poorly in school. Studying with him or her and encouraging him or her can be a loving Christian service.

If you are a teenager or young adult, how about helping others to resist peer pressure. Take a firm stand for self-discipline and good moral values. You will be teased and criticized but you are the one to whom others will later come for support. You will hear them say, "I'm in trouble. Please help me." Good example and strong moral principles can go a long way in serving others.

In the adult world also, there are many ways to serve. Of course, there are endless opportunities around the family and the home, and this can be a full time job away from your employment, but there are also many fine opportunities to serve in your employment.

For example, a man who is supervisor at a large company recently told me that where he works there are many goof-offs who, once they are on the payroll, can't be counted on to do their jobs. On the job, resisting the pressure to loaf or to steal from the company can be a fine employee ministry.

And at election time, encouraging others to vote and helping them get to the polling places or to vote absentee can be a patriotic and Christian thing to do.

It is said that virtue is its own reward. Of course, it is true that the warm feeling of satisfaction in having done something worthwhile makes us want to do more, but it goes much farther than that. Once we have crossed over into eternity, we will see very clearly how far a lifetime of serving others has brought us.

Jesus taught us that those who aspire after greatness in his kingdom must serve the needs of all. We Christians serve, not to achieve rank and recognition for ourselves, but to promote the good of others. We strive to serve with love and with a personal touch.

Something that Sister Anthony taught us as Juniors and Seniors in high school fifty years ago still sticks with me today. She encouraged the personal touch by teaching us to dedicate our individual good deeds to Jesus by saying, "This is for you, Jesus." This is a way to give every little thing we do a real purpose.

So often we base our decisions about what to do and what to avoid on the question, "Is it a sin or not?" A much better attitude for us as servants of the Lord Jesus would be, "What would he want me to do?" It's like saying on the one hand, "Do I have to?" and on the other hand, "What else do you have for me to do?"

According to the Scriptural account of the last judgment, we will all be judged on how well we served our neighbors. You see, in serving our neighbors, we serve Christ.

As in everything else, repetition builds habits and serving others can become the most Christian habit of all.

We can easily see from these thoughts why he willingly devoted his life to serving and ministering to so many other people.

Dot Harper and her husband, Deacon Linard Harper, were very good friends of Fr. Charles. She told us about an interesting side of him. She was a teacher at St. Joseph Catholic School in Yoakum. She often took her students to see Fr. Charles because he had a special ability to relate to youngsters. She said the students were always inspired by his kindness and patience and joyfulness even when he was so handicapped. They saw that people could achieve many things and maintain their composure even in spite of unusual hardships. One thing that Mrs. Harper admired about Fr. Charles was the fact that he was so grateful for the children's visits. She always had the children write him to thank him for spending some time with them. Here are two letters he wrote to the children after their visits.

Thursday, February 25, 1988

Dear Students,

I received your letters and read every one of them before I went to bed. I was very happy to hear from you and I remember meeting some of you in the hospital. I also remember visiting some of the ones you mentioned who were patients here, and praying with them and giving the Anointing of the Sick. No one likes to be sick, but if you ever have to be a patient in the hospital, I would look you up and come to see you. Would you like that?

I knew that some of you have come to Mass in the chapel on Sunday. Sometimes babies come and they cry at times, but that is their way of praying.

I was surprised to hear that you knew that I am the Fire Department Chaplain. I do not go to fires but I do attend their oyster fries, barbecues, and Christmas parties. They come and get me in a blue van. You probably have seen it parked on the hospital parking lot.

I hope you are all doing well in school and will not have to spend many years in the fifth grade. Don't worry if you don't know yet what you want to be when you grow up. Just try hard to do everything well every day, and at home, when your mother tells you to do something, don't frown and say, "Oh, Mom," but surprise your parents sometimes by hugging them or telling them you love them, and by offering to do things for them.

Now let me tell you that as a souvenir of this happy occasion I am sending each of you and your teachers a pencil, a button, two balloons, and two telephone stickers. Notice that the name printed on them is "Yoakum Catholic Hospital," but the name has now been changed to "Yoakum Community Hospital."

Now let me close by thanking you for writing and by wishing you the best of the best, and many blessings. If you come to the hospital sometime, be sure to look me up and tell me who you are.

Sincerely with love,

Father Kram

May 1, 1990

Dear Students,

Thank you very much for writing. Receiving letters from you was one of the nicest things that has happened to me lately. You gave me the impression that you really care.

I am sixty years old now and graduated from the twelfth grade in 1946 in Shiner, but I still remember how it felt to be in the fifth grade.

I lived on a farm and had a dog and a bicycle and wore overalls.

We also had a creek in which I went fishing for perch. I dug worms for bait and used a cane pole for a rod. We had lots of cane poles growing along the road. In the creek there were also frogs and snakes.

I have a brother and a sister and eleven nephews and nieces. One of them has gone to heaven, and so have my mother and father, but I am not sad because we loved each other very much and they are all praying for us.

I think you will be interested to know that I am a happy person. I like to say Mass and preach homilies and give the Sacraments and visit and pray with the patients. If you ever have to be in the hospital, I will come to see you too.

Now let me tell you a joke. A boy told a little girl, "There is no Santa Claus." The little girl replied, "Oh, yes there is." He said, "Oh yeah, how do you know?" She said, "Because the Easter Rabbit told me so."

Finally, let me close with thanks and best wishes to you all. Please keep up the good work. Let's pray for one another.

Sincerely with love,

Father Kram

P.S. I am sending you some presents to share among your-selves. I hope you like them.

Father had a way with children, didn't he?

He also had a way with the personnel in the Yoakum Fire Department. He felt honored when he was named chaplain of the department. It came about through his work at the hospital as he ministered to the patients brought to the Emergency Room by the paramedics. He always met the ambulance at the E.R. and minis-tered to the patients and their families and friends. Soon the ambu-lance personnel were seeking his counsel and consolation. "Father, do you have a minute?" or "Father, can I talk to you? I have a problem." He always took time to listen and to soothe their fears and feelings and frustrations. It wasn't long before word spread throughout the Fire Department about this remarkable minister. Through that association he was invited to be their chaplain. He offered prayers at their social events and attended their training sessions when he could. It was not unusual to see one or two members in a huddle with Father in his room or in the hall at the hospital or even in the chapel as Father listened to their problems and offered his scholarly counsel. They responded favorably to his cheerful encouragement. He even had a Fire Department badge that read: "Father Kram, Fire Chaplain, Yoakum V.F.D."

One of the members of the department, Walter Squyres, Jr., gave us these thoughts on Fr. Kram:

> I worked for the Yoakum Fire Department when Elmer Hanna was the Fire Chief. Chief Hanna thought very highly of Fr. Kram, as I did. Chief would invite Father to our various functions. Father would accept and Chief Hanna would have the men take the ambulance to the hospital to pick up Father. Father would be ready at the door of the hospital with a big smile and he'd always tell the men how glad he was to see them. At that time the firemen also served as EMS and so Father got to know them quite well.
>
> Father would bless the food we were about to eat and he asked God's blessings on the men as they went about their duties. He always thanked God for the many blessings that he gave us every day.
>
> Father Kram was one of those people you looked for when you came through the Emergency Room door with someone who needed help. He would be there praying for them and their families. He was especially important to us when we brought in someone who was dying as he had such a special way of comforting and consoling people.
>
> Father Kram was a wonderful man. He was my friend. Our community lost someone special when he went to be with the Lord.

Another member of the fire department offered these thoughts:

My name is David Ferry. I knew Fr. Kram through the Yoakum hospital. Father touched the lives of many people at the hospital. He was there because that's where he lived and where he worked. He was there for the patients and their families and for the hospital personnel. I was an Emergency Medical Technician, a Fireman, and later, the Fire Chief. Father was a large part of my life. He made it possible for me to become a Catholic. My work hours were very irregular and it was impossible for me to attend regular instructions for becoming a Catholic. Father was considerate enough to give me instructions whenever I could get to the hospital to meet with him. He made it possible for my son and me to make our First Communion together. That was a special moment for both of us.

As Fire Department Chaplain, Father attended many of our functions. He also sold raffle tickets for our fundraisers and donated items for our auctions. But, most of all, Father gave so much of himself to others. Our families loved him and our children looked forward to helping him celebrate Mass. He was so kind and thoughtful of others. We sure miss him.

In 1987, the fire department personnel converted a golf cart into an emergency medical service patrol vehicle for use at the Papal Mass by Pope John Paul II when he visited San Antonio. Father Charles blessed the cart prior to its trip to San Antonio for the glorious papal visit.

Another community ministry in which Fr. Charles was involved was one called "Dial-A-Friend." This was a group of Good Samaritans whose faith impelled them to do a good service for others. In their particular case, every day they each called several senior citizens or disabled individuals who lived alone to be sure that they were okay. At one time they had forty shut-ins to whom they ministered. Father Charles kept the records on their activities from January 1989 until he died in 2000.

He also operated a relief fund to assist the poor with the cost of medications. He used funds donated to him for this purpose.

He was always encouraging the young members of the community and supporting their activities. In 1987, the Yoakum High School's chapter of Future Homemakers of America honored him as their "Hero of the Year" for his generous support.

In 1984, the Diocese of Victoria organized its first spiritual and theological formation program leading to the ordination of worthy men to the Sacrament of Holy Orders in the Diaconate. This program was under the capable direction of Father (now Monsignor and diocesan Vicar General) John C. Peters. He was assisted by Deacon Linard Harper and Dot Harper. Through the relationship of Fr. Charles with the Harpers, who had known him and helped him with assistance at Mass, Fr. Charles developed a keen interest in the diaconate formation program. He provided funds from his personal account for the purchase of video equipment to aid in the instruction and practice of homiletics (the preparation and delivery of homilies or sermons). He also provided the funds to purchase the dalmatic vestments for the newly ordained deacons of that initial class. Six men and their wives completed the formation program.

It seems fitting that we close this chapter with these thoughts from three people who distinguished themselves by the lives they lived.

"The best way to find yourself is to lose yourself in the service of others."
    ~ Mahatma Gandhi

"The first question which the priest and the Levite asked was: 'If I stop to help this man, what will happen to me?' But the Good Samaritan reversed the question; 'If I do not stop to help this man, what will happen to him?'"
    ~ Dr. Martin Luther King, Jr.

"At the end of life we will not be judged by how many diplomas we have received, how much money we have made, how many great things we have done. We will be judged by 'I was hungry, and you gave me something to eat, I was naked and you clothed me. I was homeless, and you took me in.'"

~ Blessed Teresa of Calcutta

CHAPTER ELEVEN

Humor

Be hospitable to one another without complaining. As each one has received a gift, use it to serve one another as good stewards of God's varied grace. (1 Peter 4:9–10)

Father Charles Kram, Jr., had a lively sense of humor, even in his youth, as mentioned in Chapter One, where we heard from childhood friends about his card tricks and his production of *The Greatest Swimming Match* and *Walking on Water*. We also heard about his hilarious comparison of himself to Archbishop Fulton J. Sheen during Bishop Grahmann's stories about their times together in the seminary. Father Kram was an admirer of Archbishop Sheen, whose enormously popular radio ministry *The Catholic Hour* ran from 1930 to 1950, and whose award-winning television ministry *Life is Worth Living* aired from 1951 to 1957. It was Archbishop Sheen who opined, "Humor is closely related to faith."

The archbishop also once commented, "Hearing nuns' confessions is like being stoned to death with popcorn."

Father Charles had his own funny story about confession. In repeating it, we do not mean to be irreverent.

> Here's what happened to a newly ordained young priest on the day he heard confessions for the first time. He had just been assigned to a parish where the pastor was a seasoned old Irish Monsignor. On Saturday afternoon the two priests went to the church and took their places in the confessionals opposite each other in the back of the

church. The young priest had just made himself comfortable when a man came in and said, "Bless me, Father, for I have sinned. I got drunk twice, I beat my wife twice, and I cussed twenty times." The young priest was about to give the man a penance and a bit of advice when the man interrupted him and said, "And Father, there's something else I guess I ought to tell you. That is, I hate to say it, Father, but I'm a bootlegger." At this the inexperienced young priest panicked because he had no idea what kind of penance to give a bootlegger. So he got up and tiptoed over to the other side to get a bit of advice from the Monsignor. He said, "Monsignor, I've got a bootlegger in my box. What shall I give him?" The monsignor gave it five seconds of serious thought and then replied, "I wouldn't be giving the lad more than $1.35 a pint."

Then there's the story he told about marriage. Sometimes our attempts at faith come up against obstacles. For example, at a class reunion one classmate asked another, "Frank, why didn't you ever marry?" and Frank replied, "I brought home five wonderful girls and showed them to my parents, but my mother didn't like any of them. Finally, I found a girl who looked like my mother, she talked like my mother, she walked like her and she acted like her. My mother approved her, but I couldn't marry her because my father didn't like her." So there you have it. Life is full of obstacles.

Dot Harper, who taught religion to the third, fourth, and fifth grade classes at St. Joseph Catholic School in Yoakum, was a good friend of Fr. Charles. She often took the students to see Father when they were studying the sacraments and he would give them interesting presentations on administering the sacraments wherein he had the students act as his hands in the demonstrations. A close bond had developed between Fr. Charles and Mrs. Harper. She tells this funny story: "At one point in my life, I had just been to the beauty shop and had a permanent and my hair was fluffy, and he said, 'Your hair looks nice. I think that must be a Bohemian Afro.'"

A favorite joke of his about hospital food went this way: "One day during the Chaplain's rounds, a patient, who had been on a liquids-only diet for days told me how pleased she was at having just had her first solid food. 'Yes,' she said, 'I saw four specks of parsley floating in my broth.' You have to find humor in ordinary moments, too."

Another favorite of his was this story about driver education: "The most valuable piece of safe-driving literature that I have ever seen was one that my older brother received at the gas station where we used to fill up our 1929 Chevy back in the 1930s when I was a little boy. It was a one-page booklet entitled 'Manual of Instructions for Back Seat Drivers.' The page read: 'Shut Up!'"

Good advice.

Here are a couple of dialogues he dreamed up for his entertainment and that of others:

The Making of a Missionary
By Father Charles Kram

This is the story of the adventures of an aging padre and his efforts to acquaint himself with the needs of his people. He is not someone any of us might know personally, we hope. The adventures, as told by the subject himself, were as follows:

Last Sunday after Mass, I was sitting around the rectory, congratulating myself on the wonderful sermon I had preached on brotherhood and love of neighbor, when a sudden thought struck me. I said to myself, "Father, maybe you ought to take a drive around the area and get to know some of the people out there." What I meant was, "Father, it could well be that you're too middle-class-affluent-conservative and maybe if you were to run up against some hard-core-liberal radicals or something, the experience might balance you up just right and make you an informed, relevant, involved sort of padre." Already I was beginning to see myself as some kind of modern-day St. Paul—someone for everyone.

So, if I were going, the first thing I had to do was decide what to wear. I said to myself, "Father, you don't want to look too worldly and unrecognizable as a clergyman, but at the same time, you don't want to look too stuffy and unapproachable." It was a hot day, so I finally settled for one of those white-collar black shirts with short sleeves. They look professional, yet sporty and fashionable, and, besides, I always did look good in basic black, and even more so now since it goes well with the grey hairs on my venerable old head. Furthermore, I've never known Church regulations to penalize a padre for being handsome.

So, off to the garage I went, and almost got into the Lincoln Town Car when a quiet little voice inside my conscience said to me, "If you expect to be believable about the spirit of detachment and voluntary poverty and all that, go in the Chevrolet." So I meditated for a moment on Matthew 23:28, about hypocrisy and iniquity, and even though the Chevrolet didn't have stereo, I got into it and drove down the street.

After a while, the neighborhood began to look a little unfamiliar to me, so I stopped and asked a policeman whether I was still in my parish, but he just frowned and said, "Huh?" and told me to ask another priest. A smart remark like that makes it hard even for a man of my quality to control his temper, but after meditating for a moment on 1 Peter 3:9, about not returning insult for insult but returning a blessing instead, I pulled myself together and said to the policeman, "Oh, bless you, Officer," and quickly drove off. I said to myself, "So that's what police brutality feels like."

So I drove on until I came to a spot where there was a small park, and there I saw two men beating up a woman. I got out and shook my finger at them and told them, "I'm a clergyman and that's not the Christian thing to do," but they just laughed at me and ran off with the poor woman's purse. I said to myself, "Father, it's no use reporting this incident to the police; they'll just insult you and tell you to tell another priest." So I helped the unfortunate victim to her feet and gave her the rectory phone number and assured her that my secretary would help get her another purse. My scriptural basis for this was Luke 10:33 about the Good Samaritan.

About that time a sick-looking man walked up to me and asked me whether I needed a fix. I couldn't think of anything that needed fixing just then, and besides, the parish has too darn many maintenance agreements already, so I told the man, "We priests like to favor the little man, but at the time diocesan policy requires dealing only with people with established reputations." The poor man seemed to have an emotional reaction when I told him this, but even in his weakened condition, he seemed to understand. My action was fully in accord with Luke 16:2 about responsible stewardship.

So I got back into my car and had gone hardly a block when I noticed two attractive young ladies waving to me and motioning me to stop. I said to myself, "They probably noticed I'm a priest and probably want to know the schedule for confessions and Sunday Mass," but the way it turned out, they were selling something and wanted to do business with me. I couldn't quite figure out what firm they represented, so I also gave them the rectory phone number and assured them that my secretary would be happy to give them her opinion. This solution was based on our policy of equal opportunity for women and against discrimination based on gender.

Finally, in consideration of Matthew 11:19, I had one more stop to make. "My mission is to the publicans and sinners," I said. "And since they don't go to church, it's up to me to go where they are." About that time I saw a sign that read "MOTEL," so I pulled in and went inside. I didn't want anyone to think I was a corrupt padre or something, and besides, I wasn't sure which motels were corrupt, so I stretched the truth a little and said to the man at the desk, "I'm doing research for my new book about corruption among the clergy and I'm looking for a sleazy motel. Is this a sleazy motel?" Instead of trying to be helpful, the man very rudely hustled me out the door and slammed it behind me. I could see that I wasn't welcome, so in accordance with Matthew 10:14, I shook the dust off my feet and hurried back to the car.

As I drove back to the rectory, I said to myself, "Father, be thankful you're called to be a priest, instead of being caught up in the rudeness and irresponsibility and confusion of our sinful world and that you have been given intelligence and sound judgment and a good understanding of mankind's deepest needs."

It was at that point that the inspiration struck me to preach next Sunday on the subject of loving one's neighbor as oneself but not instead of oneself, or something like that, if I can find a text on which to base it.

The second one is much like the first.

New Capsule About to Hit Market
By Father Charles Kram

Having been a hospital chaplain since 1977, I thought I had heard everything, but I was wrong. Have you heard the latest pill news? Hoax-Charlatan Pharmaceuticals, Inc., has just announced the development of what they claim to be the ultimate cure for hypochondria.

Hypochondria is defined as unhealthy anxiety about one's health with the thinking up of phony ailments. It can take many forms, but the new remedy has proven to be effective against them all.

Basically, the new product is not new; rather, it is an improvement on an old tried-and-true common remedy for hypochondria, the common placebo.

The ordinary placebo consists of a worthless, harmless, useless substance usually in pill form, which, if taken as directed, will alleviate the imaginary ailments of the hypochondriac at least temporarily.

The breakthrough which we are discussing here takes the pill one step farther and provides the same thing in the form of a time release capsule that seeps the above mentioned substances into the system little by little so as to maintain a therapeutic level in the bloodstream over an extended period of time, without dangerous peaks or troughs.

The new product will be marketed under the trade name "KHONDRIKAP" and will sell for a price high enough to convince the patient that there is something to it, and it will be available only by prescription—otherwise, how could you expect your insurance to cover it?

A spokesman for the manufacturer has already expressed fears that as soon as the FDA has finished testing their new product on monkeys and it hits the human market, the generic drug mills will start grinding out cheap imitations with which to flood the market. That is what has already happened to cigarettes and beer and crankcase oil.

KHONDRIKAP capsules will be available as either red and white or green and white because a color difference can give the impression that there is a real difference, and this can be important to a product's effectiveness, especially with patients who take delight in publicizing their pill consumption. Being able to say, "My doctor had to put me on the stronger ones" can sometimes spell the difference between mere improvement and truly meeting the patient's needs.

What about danger of overdose, toxicity, and addictiveness? As we have already stated, KHONDRIKAP capsules have no drug-related contents and therefore can have no side effects. As one hypochondriologist put it, "There is more likelihood that Niagara Falls will one day fall upwards, than that anyone will ever be hurt by this effective new product." What could be safer than that? The capsules will not even come in child-proof containers.

A final question: "Who should take the new capsule?" Probably the best answer is that it doesn't really matter, but if you think you need them, take a copy of this article with you the next time you see your doctor. He will tell you what he thinks.

Here are several more of Fr. Charles's humorous stories:

As a present for his sixth birthday, little David's parents gave him a wallet with a few dollars in it. His mother advised him to fill in the identification card just in case he lost the wallet. He dutifully did so.

Later, when she checked to see whether the boy had done it right, she found everything to be in order, except that in the space requesting his blood type, he had entered "red."

Once, during her teaching career, my friend Shelly asked her class of alert five-year-olds whether anyone could name a season of the year. One of the little girls enthusiastically threw up her hand and volunteered, "Deer season."

One morning in the hospital where I was being cared for, an attractive pinafore-clad student nurse appeared in my room and told me that she had been assigned to be my nurse that day. The reason she gave was that the patient to whom she had first been assigned had died.

Don, the barber who trims my hair, tells of the bitter cold he had to endure as an infantryman in Korea in the 1950s.

He claims that one night it was so cold that a snowman tried to wedge himself into his foxhole with him.

When Fr. Charles noticed how apprehensive small children were about being patients in the hospital, he compiled a booklet of positive stories complete with cartoons illustrated by Patsey Macmelugiin. It was a big hit with the little ones. The stories went like this:

A lazy little turtle
Kept sleeping on a rock
He said he had no reason
To ever watch the clock.

A flashy little goldfish
Kept swimming in his bowl
He said that being idle
Never was his goal.

A happy little chicken
Kept cackling on her nest
And every time she laid an egg
She laid her very best.

A frisky little kitten
Kept chasing birds for fun
Until a huge canary
Put her on the run.

A little bunny rabbit
Kept hopping to and fro
He said it was the motion
That kept him on the go.

A noisy little squirrel
Kept climbing high for nuts
He always chattered loudly
For his work took guts.

A jumpy little froggie
Kept splashing in a pond
He said it felt delightful
Of water he was fond.

A slender little serpent
Would doze along a limb
He couldn't doze across it
Because he was too slim.

Among all the papers contributed to the archive of Fr. Charles's memorabilia is a cartoon he drew and dated May 19, 1967. He then gave it to his cousin Elton Zander. It shows two ranchers examining a short-legged, long-bodied horse. One rancher is speaking to the other and says, "This breed is what we call a *Dachshorse*."

We must keep in mind that his drawings were done with a pencil attached to a long stick he held in his mouth since he was unable to use his hands.

When the Pink Ladies' Auxiliary of the Yoakum Community Hospital compiled a book of favorite recipes in 2010, they included a favorite recipe of Fr. Charles. It was as follows:

Holey Egg
In memory of Fr. Charles Kram

1 egg	Butter
1 slice bread	Salt and Pepper

(This recipe is not holy or sacred or blessed but is "holey" because its name is derived from the fact that to make it you first remove the center of a slice of bread so as to make a hole about two inches in diameter.) Spread butter on both sides of the slice and place it into a frying pan. Break the egg into the hole and fry until firm. Turn slice over and fry until done. Add pepper, salt, and syrup or jelly. Serve with bacon or breakfast sausage. Use the leftover center of the slice as a nutritious mop to clean your plate.

It is a well-known fact of life that laughter is one of the strongest and most effective medicines for the body and soul. An old Yiddish proverb tells us: "What soap is to the body, laughter is to the soul."

Health care researchers readily agree that a lively and healthy sense of humor goes a long way toward easing stress and stimulating the effective functioning of the heart and the immune system and one's mental faculties. A good laugh simply makes us feel good.

Most of us are familiar with the very popular "Laughter Is the Best Medicine" section of the *Reader's Digest*. That section undoubtedly helped make the publication such a success for so many years.

There is an old Irish Proverb that says it this way: "A good laugh and a long sleep are the best cures in the Doctor's Book."

Father Charles knew and understood that truth very well.

CHAPTER TWELVE

Writings and Homilies

When the Pharisees heard that he had silenced the Sadducees, they gath-
ered together, and one of them (a scholar of the law) tested him by asking,
"Teacher, which commandment in the law is the greatest?" He said to him,
"You shall love the Lord, your God, with all your heart, with all your soul,
and with all your mind. This is the greatest and the first commandment. The
second is like it; you shall love your neighbor as yourself. The whole law and
the prophets depend on these two commandments." (Matthew 22:34–40)

Father Charles thought and lived according to all the teachings of Jesus and his holy Church, but his love of God and neighbor shines forth like a beacon, especially in his writings and homilies. We cannot present them all here, but we can offer a few as examples.

ON EDUCATION IN A CATHOLIC SCHOOL

I was a member of the Senior Class of 1946 at St. Ludmila's Academy. Our class of seven boys and six girls graduated from SLA near the mid-point of the twentieth century, fifty years ago last year.

Let me describe SLA as it was then. The main structure was the three-story brick building that is still in use today, in which our high school classes were held and in which the Sisters lived. To the north stood an old three-story wooden building for the elementary grades. There was, at the time, no gym and St. Paul's was not even a twinkle in anyone's eye. The only organized sport consisted of the SLA Cardinals' basketball team, which was at the time only two years old.

All of the teachers were nuns dressed in full habits with ankle-length skirts and wide veils and with the biggest rosaries you ever saw dangling from their waists. We had great respect for them and whenever we would meet one, we would say, "Praised be Jesus Christ, Sister."

The one person who most influenced our lives as teenagers was our principal, Sister Anthony, the person most often mentioned whenever our old classmates meet. What she lacked in size, she made up in spiritual clout. When she spoke, we listened. Whenever we would disappoint her, she would hold her head in her hands and say, "Bozi," which in Czech means "God."

She instilled the fear and especially the love of God into our hearts to stay and in return, we helped make her a saint.

As compared to the teenagers of today, we had far simpler challenges to meet and far less peer pressure to face. There were no illegal drugs or teenage drinking. No teenager owned a car and there was little money to spend. Modesty in speech and in dress was the norm.

Our families were our strength. We ate together and went visiting together and attended movies and dances and Mass together and since many of us lived on farms, we often also worked together.

How quickly the world changes and how quickly we change with it. Whether things get better or worse depends very largely on the quality of what each generation hands down to the next.

The starting place is in the family and the home. What the family cannot do alone is entrusted to the school, which must be able to teach the children according to the parents' wishes.

The philosophy that is in vogue today in public education teaches that there is no fixed standard of morality, but that right and wrong are whatever you choose them to be. This leaves God out of the picture and undermines authority of every kind.

In schools like ours we are free to put God back in everything we do and to teach good moral and religious values, to invoke God's name and promote school and home prayer, to celebrate our religious feasts and display symbols of our faith on the wall.

Our schools can instill a sense of personal worth and can teach habits of personal responsibility and self-control.

And where modern history books have been rewritten to downplay national heroes who have inspired us for generations past, we can write them back in and add the role models of our choice from our own spiritual Hall of Fame.

Yes, we need all kinds of help if we are to mature. Consider that even lions have to teach their cubs how to roar.

Just to illustrate what happens when no one is allowed to set the standards, one educator had the theory that if you let the children themselves make the rules, they will end up with high moral values and the discipline problem will solve itself. His theory turned out to be a complete failure. He found that in each case, the standards of the group turned out to be those of the worst members. Bad companions do bring out the worst in us.

Besides the freedom to teach the things in which we believe, what else gives our school an advantage over many of their public counterparts?

One elementary school teacher told me that one thing she especially likes in the Catholic elementary school in which she teaches is the unusual harmony she sees between parents and teachers. The teachers as well as the parents are mostly all local people who plan to stay in the community. They all know each other and when there is a project or a problem, they all want to help. The school is theirs, and since it represents a considerable personal and financial investment, they want to see it succeed.

A man I know recently told me that he attended a Catholic school for only one year of his life. "Tuition was three dollars a month and my parents couldn't afford it," he said. Now, according to figures the local pastor gave me, the cost is almost a hundred times as great.

Is it worth that much?

Let me tell you how one dad looked at it. He said that instead of saving his money to leave to his children when he died and perhaps have them spend it on something of little importance, he was spending it now to give them the best education he could afford. In this way, he was giving them something that they could never lose and that no one could take away from them.

In my day SLA gave me an education that was altogether adequate for the needs of the times, but more importantly, I learned the great value of love and self-sacrifice and of keeping my life centered on Christ. These things have meant so much to me.

The Catholic schools used to be looked down upon. Now they are looked up to as the place to go for all the essentials of what a sound secular and religious education should be, and as a bonus, the children get a strong witness to their faith.

Are we not proud?

So, thanks, Sisters, and congratulations to SLA and St. Paul's and all the other Catholic schools out there that are working very hard to show our people how to live our lives according to the will of God.

ON COMPLAINING

Complaining is such a popular sport. It is easy to do and it is fun. It gets things off our chests. It helps to strike out against persons and things we resent.

But it also spreads ill will and discontent. It breaks up harmony among our friends and peers. It disrupts long-standing relationships.

Chronic complainers are never satisfied. They generate their own unhappiness. They lose the respect of those who have to listen to them. And since complaining requires no willpower, they are left with feelings of guilt for giving in to their weakness.

So, if you must complain, complain constructively. Complain to build up rather than to tear down. Turn your complaint around and ask yourself, "If this complaint were about me, would it help me or would it hurt me?"

Above all, let God help you. He does not need us but he does help us if we help ourselves.

ON CHAIN LETTERS

Like me, you have probably at one time or another received a chain letter. Such letters tend to have certain things in common, such as a report about the number of times they have been around the world, instructions to send out a certain number of copies before a deadline, and the reports of good or bad luck that keep them going.

Chain letters are like a plague, but they spread only as long as the persons who receive them make copies. If you should receive a chain letter, don't hesitate to throw it away.

Break the chain. Otherwise, you make yourself a necessary link in an ever-expanding pyramid of fear and superstition.

We Christians do not live by luck but by the kind Providence of a loving Father. Nothing escapes his control. If we trust him, he will take care of us.

So, can chain letters hurt you? The answer is yes, but only if you choose to make yourself a part of them. Breaking the chain is an act of love toward all those whom fear and superstition might have victimized.

Break the chain.

ON PRAYER

I dedicate this to everyone who believes in the power of prayer.

So much harm is done by worry and doubt and so much good is done by faith and by prayer backed up by a strong faith.

Anyone can be a prophet of doom but anyone can also be a prophet of prosperity and of good days ahead. Prophecies of either kind tend to be self-fulfilling because they affect our way of thinking and of acting and of spreading our feelings, and they certainly affect the strength of our faith.

Peter walked on water until he doubted. Then he sank. Jesus was disappointed in him and asked him why he had faltered. If we doubt, we sink.

Once when a Canaanite woman asked Jesus for a favor, he said no, because she was an outsider and it wouldn't be right to throw the children's food to the dogs. So the woman asked for table scraps. Her faith and perseverance pleased Jesus so much that he promptly granted her request, assuring her that the evil spirit had already left her sick little child.

Where Jesus is concerned, we are by no means outsiders. We belong to him more than any other people could and we have a high claim on his favors, provided that we have faith.

Faith is so important that the miracle-working powers of Jesus were seriously hindered in his own native place for no other reason than the people there did not believe in him. Faith could have brought his own people their full share of wonders.

James says that we must ask in faith, never doubting, and that the doubter must not expect to receive anything from the Lord.

Faith is also a gift to be asked for, so first pray for a strong faith. Then pray as one filled with the joyful expectation that the prayer is already on the way. Crowd out every fear or doubt or negative thought with something positive and encouraging and make a strong reaffirmation of faith, like "Everything will turn out all right" or "Lord, I used to doubt, but not anymore."

To ask when we wish to receive implies that the less we ask, the less we will receive. God is lavish with his gifts, but he wants to be asked. Ask a great deal.

Worrying indicates a lack of faith and accomplishes nothing useful. In fact, why should the worrier ever bother to pray?

A man once complained to God and asked him why he was taking so long to answer his prayers. God told him, "My child, I couldn't help because you just wouldn't let go."

It has been said that one thing that we, God's children, owe to our beloved Father is not ever to be afraid of anything. "Do not be afraid, little flock, for the Father has been pleased to give you the Kingdom."

A simple prayer that anyone can say over and over throughout the day is, "Jesus, I love you." The simple expression of
love can be given as many meanings as there are feelings in
the human heart; "I love you," "I let go," "I abandon myself
to you," "I'm sad today and I just wanted you to know,"
"I'll hang on until you rescue me."

Instead of worrying, then, let's all ask our Father for a
strong faith, then let's pray with a firm faith. Do it often
and do it without faltering.

Any time and every time you feel a worry or a doubt or a
cloud of gloom, quickly say, "Jesus, I love you."

You will be heard.

ODE TO A HOLY NIGHT

In a land afar, beneath a star in Israel

Was born a Son, the Promised One Emmanuel.

Though long foretold by prophets old this humble guest

Of men the least with stabled beasts chose first to rest.

The Angels sang, their *Glorias* rang and filled the night.

The shepherds feared, then hastened near the manger site.

They knelt to pray, for in the hay, in sweet repose

Lay David's Son, the Holy One, the Christmas Rose.

O World forlorn! What joyous morn this Babe foretells.

Forsake your fear. The Christ is here. Let ring your bells.

O ageless Lord, in crib adored, I worship Thee.

For Thou art King, in clothes swaddling, for love of me.

ON DEPENDENCY

We live in a world in which no creature is an island, in which all of us are interdependent, and in the case of us humans, a world in which the freely chosen actions and omissions of each of us help or hinder the rest of us. In fact, it is especially in the world of humans that we find the greatest variety of rivalries and competitions and balancing acts.

We humans like to belong. We do not like to sit at home alone. Living in the spiritual world as well as in the material, we need one another more than any other species. We fight on two fronts, and our position can bring out either the best or the worst in us.

But our Christian calling impels us to serve the needs of one another. Jesus made this very clear when he settled an argument among his followers about who was to be the greatest in his kingdom. He told them that anyone who wished to be great among them must serve the rest.

Think about this. Sooner or later any one of us could come to the point of being ill or disabled or broke, and dependent on others for many things that we were used to doing for ourselves. We don't like the thought of it. Sometimes we can't help but accept the help of others.

Dependency can be harder to bear than the ailment that caused it. Having to rely on others can turn a bully into a crybaby. It can make you bitter or make you better. It can make you a sinner or a saint.

Those who have to depend on others might well consider that many a good deed would have to be left undone, were it not for such special needs. Gracious acceptance promotes devoted service. A famous quote from the poet John Milton says, "He also serves who only stands and waits."

We can all live and grow and help one another live and grow by directly helping one another, but we must also seek strength through prayers. Don't let us forget that all things come from God, and with God's help we can do all things.

While we depend on one another, our greatest dependency is on God.

ON THE ANNUNCIATION

In worldly terms, Mary never did anything spectacular. She was not rich or powerful. She was not known far and wide. She was of no consequence. She was just a simple virgin girl who was willing always to follow God's will wherever he might wish to lead her. Yet her life was extremely meaningful. She was a key person in salvation history, a person whom all generations still call blessed.

The reason for her greatness was not by her choice. Rather, God chose HER for the greatest privilege ever bestowed on any woman, the blessing that every Israelite maiden would have cherished, to be the mother of the Messiah.

She did not aspire after it. She did not expect it. Even when the angel announced it, she did not understand it. But she accepted it. By God's choice and by her acceptance, it was accomplished.

Mary is a true VIP in God's plan of salvation, and she knows Jesus better than anyone else who ever lived. There is so much of Mary in Jesus. She conceived him and she gave him birth. She fed him and clothed him and gave him a home. She taught him how to walk and how to talk. She was with him in his triumph and in his shame. She was present at every significant event of his life.

She was there when Gabriel announced that she would conceive and bear a son.

She was there when she rejoiced with her cousin Elizabeth over the special blessings she had received.

She was there on that holy night when the angels sang and she laid his infant form in his manger bassinet.

She was there at the Presentation of Jesus in the Temple when Simeon prophesied that a sword would pierce her soul.

She was there searching for him and finding him in the Temple when he was twelve years old.

She was there at the wedding feast of Cana where Jesus worked his first public miracle, changing water into wine, and then she was present during his entire public ministry witnessing his miracles as he mingled with the crowd.

She was there at the foot of the cross when Jesus died and she received his lifeless body into her arms.

She was there to see the empty tomb.

She was with the Apostles as a living witness to the Resurrection and she was there in the Upper Room praying with them while they waited for the coming of the Holy Spirit.

Finally, she was there on Pentecost day to see the parted tongues of fire and the birthday of the Church.

Mary has gone all the way with Jesus here on earth, from the beginning to the end.

So, to me, Mary is the perfect disciple, the first among the faithful, the model of all Christians, indeed, the most privileged woman in all history.

And, it all began with the Annunciation as told in the Gospel according to Luke 1:26–38.

ON THE EUCHARIST

The Eucharist has a long and interesting history, made up of many parts, dating all the way back to Abraham.

As described in Genesis 14, at the time of Abraham there was a priest king named Melchizedek. He was King of Salem, later named Jerusalem, which became the center of the Jewish faith and the symbol of the new Jerusalem, the kingdom of the Messiah. Melchizedek was also a priest. Instead of animal sacrifices, Melchizedek offered sacrifices in bread and wine.

Psalm 110 describes the Messiah as a King and a Priest: "The Lord swore an oath and he will not repent; You are a priest forever, according to the order of Melchizedek."

Melchizedek was a prototype of Christ, who was a king and a priest, who at the Last Supper offered bread and wine.

Another part of history of the Eucharist is found in Genesis 22, in the story of Abraham and Isaac. Abraham had an only son, Isaac. God would call Abraham to a very special destiny in the future of his people. To test him he told him to slay his son and offer him in sacrifice. Abraham did not understand but he obeyed God without question. He took fire and wood for the holocaust and started out for the hill that God had shown him. He laid the wood for the sacrifice on Isaac's shoulders and had him carry it up the hill. Isaac asked his father, "Father, where is the victim for the sacrifice?" Abraham, still trusting God, told him, "God himself will supply the victim." Abraham built an altar, laid the wood on it, tied up his son, laid him on the altar, and took the knife to slaughter him. Then an angel came and told Abraham not to lay a hand on his son. Then Abraham looked around and saw a ram caught by its horns in a thicket, and he sacrificed it in place of his son.

God had given Abraham a test (in obedience) and because of his loyalty, God made a covenant with him: "Your descendants shall be as countless as the stars in the sky and as numerous as the grains of sand on the seashore and in you all the nations on the earth shall be blessed."

The story of Abraham and Isaac was a prototype of the sacrifice of Jesus on the cross. God supplied the Victim. The Victim was the Father's only Son. He carried the wood on his shoulders. He was sacrificed on a hill.

Another part of the history of the Eucharist is the story of the Passover, described in Exodus 12. It was the tenth and worst plague that God sent on the Egyptians so the Pharaoh would let his people go, when the angel of death struck every firstborn of the Egyptians, man and beast alike.

Through Moses, God instructed the Israelites that every family choose a year-old male lamb that had no blemish, slaughter it at twilight, and put some of its blood on their doorposts. That same night they must eat the roasted flesh of the lamb with the unleavened bread and bitter herbs.

In the morning cries and weeping were heard all over the land because all of the firstborn lay dead, but no destructive blow fell on the households marked with the blood of the lamb.

God's command to his people for the future was: "This day shall be a memorial feast for you, which all your generations shall celebrate as a perpetual institution. You must observe this rite when you have entered the land the Lord will give you." Even to this day, the Jews celebrate the Passover every year.

The sacrificial lamb of the Passover was a prototype of Jesus, the Lamb of God, whose blood would deliver his people from the slavery of sin and death. Centuries later when John the Baptist caught sight of Jesus coming toward him, he said, "Look, there is the Lamb of God who takes away the sin of the world."

Jesus ate the Passover with his disciples for the last time on the night he was betrayed. He took bread, blessed it, broke it, gave it to his disciples and said, "This is my Body, which will be given up for you." Then he took a cup, gave it to his disciples and said, "This is the cup of my blood, the blood of the New and everlasting covenant, which shall be shed for you and for all so that sins may be forgiven. Do this in memory of me."

Jesus is the bread of life. As told in Exodus 16, for forty years God fed his people manna in the desert. The Jews called it bread from heaven. In John 6, Jesus told the people, "Your ancestors ate manna in the desert and died. I am the Bread of Life. He who eats this bread shall live forever. The bread that I will give is my flesh. My flesh is real food and my blood is real drink."

In 1 Corinthians 11, Paul says, "Every time you eat this bread and drink this cup, you proclaim the death of the Lord until he comes."

If you tell me that you work in an office because you know business, or you are a housewife because you have committed yourself to marriage, or you are a rancher because you know cattle, I will tell you that I change bread and wine into the Body and Blood of Christ in memory of him because I am a priest according to the order of Melchizedek.

God takes care of his children. Just as he once delivered the children of Israel from the bondage in Egypt through the blood of the Passover lamb, so too he now delivers us, the children of the new Israel, from the bondage of sin and death through the blood of his only Son.

It is through him and with him and in him that we bring honor and glory to our Almighty Father and we pray, "Lamb of God, you take away the sins of the world, have mercy on us, grant us peace."

Lord Jesus, thank you for being our Bread of Life. Help us always to receive you worthily. Grant that, nourished by your Body and Blood, we may all live forever. Amen.

HOMILY AT HIS BROTHER'S FUNERAL

"On this day on which my brother Edgar's remains are laid to rest, I would like to contribute some thoughts of my own about death, the final fact of life.

We know not the day nor the hour. The most unavoidable and usually the most unwelcome fact of life is death. We do not even want to think about it. Sometimes, to feel more at ease, we joke about it.

Sometimes adults try to shield little children from the reality of death. A child is told that a grandparent who has died has merely gone away on a long, long trip.

When I was a little boy, my mom and dad and my brother and sister and I all attended funerals together. It taught us at an early age that death is real and final.

We must all die one day. No one is too young or too strong or too healthy to die. Even the finest doctors can't guarantee anyone a long life. And they also die.

Every generation in history had died out completely, and so will ours. A hundred years from now we will be gone and so will everything that we now struggle for and cling to.

Consider all the old abandoned farmhouses in the countryside, the rundown remains of once-thriving community settlements, the old country schoolhouses that have disappeared almost without a trace. All of these were full of life and activity only a generation ago.

Material possessions so quickly come and go, and so do we. As one poet said, "The paths of glory lead but to the grave."

Some call death the "Great Equalizer." Others call it the "Grim Reaper." General MacArthur, in his old age, called it "That Scoundrel."

From the natural viewpoint death makes no sense. It ends all our plans, it destroys all our accomplishments, it goes so far as to tear our very nature apart.

The book *Gulliver's Travels* describes a land where the inhabitants could not die. They could only grow older and older. We all want immortality but that kind of immortality would only be a curse.

Jesus, the perfect man, chose to die. He was the only man ever born to die. He did it to free us from death and give us true immortality. At the Resurrection we will all come back to life and there will be a judgment of all mankind, after which there will be only eternal reward or eternal punishment.

We need to think about death every now and then and let the thought of our own final end influence our lives for the better. Visit a cemetery sometime. Take a friend and stroll among the graves. Read the inscriptions on the stones and speculate on who the individuals were and how they might have lived and died and where their souls are now. Read the obituary every now and then. You will soon find names of people you knew, some of whom may have been much younger than you. One day someone will read your name there, too.

When we die, a mortician prepares our body for viewing. At our funeral rites a sermon praises our good deeds. Then our remains are transported to the burial site and lowered into the grave and covered with dirt. A polished stone marks our final resting place until the end of time.

Now I have a question. Should we be afraid of death? Billy Graham, when asked whether he was afraid to die, replied that he was not afraid to be dead but that he did feel a bit of apprehension about how it would happen. That seems to be about as good an answer as any for the faithful Christian.

Here's a second question. Is it wrong to want to die? Sometimes people who are in unbearable misery or pain beg God to take them. We are not permitted to take our own lives but it is not wrong to desire death as a release from unbearable burdens. Neither is it wrong to wish to leave this world to be with God. Saint Paul said that he longed to be dissolved, to be with Christ. He desired death as a means to union with God.

We know neither the day nor the hour, but if we are prepared, our death will be a most happy fate.

Now in conclusion, let me say a few words of farewell to my brother. Edgar, since you were my older brother, thanks for being a second daddy to me when I was a child.

Thanks for helping look after Mom and Dad and me during all those years after polio.

Thanks for letting me minister to you as a priest when you were ill. In life I loved and respected you. Now in death I will not forget you. Rest in peace until we meet again.

ON SUFFERING

One of the most baffling, most discouraging and most widespread problems in the whole world is the problem of evil and suffering. In fact, the origin and purpose of evil is in many ways a mystery. Why would a God who is so good make a world in which there is so much trouble?

Some would solve the problem by denying evil is real, and declare it to be an illusion of the mind. Others admit the existence of evil by denying the existence of God. Madalyn Murray O'Hare, the famous atheist, says that she cannot believe in God because of such things as tornadoes, earthquakes, and deformed babies. Still others admit both the existence of God and the existence of evil, but deny God's control over evil.

For us, the important question is, can evil be God's will? In this case, we must distinguish. Moral evil, no, because sin is so opposed to God's perfect nature, that for him it would be a contradiction. God permits sin but does not will it. If sin were to exist without God's allowing it, God would not be almighty.

But physical evil, yes, because God is Lord and Master of the universe, and has every right to have incomprehensible judgments and unsearchable ways. If a loving parent can will the pain and humiliation of a spanking, God can will disease, deformity, or natural disaster.

I am sure that no Christian would deny that there is a connection between the trials and tribulations of this world and our sins, but would it be correct to say, as one lady said to me years ago, that two of her babies were born dead perhaps because she was not properly married to their father? And would it be fair to say that those who suffer the most must have sinned the most?

The answer to both questions is no. Unless you are speaking of natural consequences of sin, such as venereal disease from romantic recklessness, or spots on the liver from alcoholic overindulgence, etc., we can say only that the misfortunes of the human race are the result of sin.

Jesus never committed the slightest sin, yet no one ever suffered like he did. Who ever sweated blood like he did? Who was ever scourged and crowned and crucified like he was? Whose heart was ever pierced by a soldier's lance like his was?

It is a fact that, all over the world, the innocent suffer along with the just. Sometimes the guilty prosper and the innocent suffer. This is one of the mysteries of suffering. Another is that the sufferings of one person can help another.

I'm sure you have all heard of the Mystical Body of Christ. Saint Paul compares the members of Christ's Church to the members of a body. Christ is the Head and we are the members. Each member has a part to play. If one member is weak or sick with sin, the whole body works to strengthen him and bring him back.

In the body of a person who has a cold, we do not say that the nose has a cold or the bronchial tubes have a cold, but the person has a cold, and the appropriate members produce fever, antibodies, and a cough, and the whole body cooperates to fight the attacker.

So, too, in the Body of Christ, when one member sins and weakens the Body, the whole Body joins in the suffering and in the rebuilding. If there were no sin, and all Christ's members were well, the whole Mystical Body would be well. Also, when any member deserves praise, the whole body rejoices. These things are true because in Christ we are one.

Jesus, as Head of the Body that is the Church, reigns gloriously in heaven. So as the Head he can no longer suffer and die. But he does still suffer every day in his members. A certain man went on a trip to a very poor country. He saw disease, ignorance, and misery. When he came back, he said, "I never saw so many Christs in my life."

It is because of this very close relationship between Christ and all the members who suffer that at the judgment, he will call the sufferers his brethren, and he will praise and reward those who have lovingly striven to help him.

In a sense, the Redemption is still going on and will not be complete until the last soul to be saved is safely in heaven.

So, suffering in itself is an evil and a curse. In the Garden of Olives, Jesus begged his Father to release him from his sufferings. Jesus faced the most terrible of sufferings, but he ended up by letting his Father have his way: "Thy will be done," he said.

Just think what if the Father had answered, "All right, my Son, I release you from your commitment. You need not suffer any more. Go in peace and be a carpenter. Let someone else be the Savior of the world."

But the Father's will and Christ's acceptance of it brought about not just the Redemption, but his glorious Resurrection and his Ascension to reign forever at his Father's right hand.

Jesus knew how to turn an evil and a curse into countless blessings. In union with him, we can do likewise. In praying for those who are suffering and encouraging and assisting them, we are doing just as St. Paul did in support of his followers. He said, "I rejoice now in the sufferings I bear for your sake, and what is lacking of the sufferings of Christ, I fill up in my flesh, for his Body, which is the Church."

O Christ, remember the compassion with which you healed the sick. Remember the special love you have for all who suffer. Remember how you chose human beings to minister in your name. Amen.

WHO AM I? WHY AM I HERE?

In the sixties, when college students were staging sit-ins and burning their buildings and kidnapping their professors, it was popular to have an identity crisis that left its victims asking, "Who am I?" and "What is my purpose in life?" and "Why do I even exist?"

To us Christians, the question of identity and purpose poses no problems. At Baptism, we each received our own Christian name that identifies us as followers of Christ. As such, we are adopted children of our Heavenly Father and heirs of heaven. Our purpose is to carry out Jesus' great commandment of love and to help spread the good news of salvation to the ends of the earth.

We are never without a calling of one kind or another.

Little children are called to learn how to talk and how to walk, how to obey and how to share, how to do all the basic things in life.

Adolescents and young adults are called to search out and prepare for their station in life.

Mature adults are called to be providers and advisers until the next generation can shoulder its responsibilities.

Those who are past their productive years also still have an important purpose in life. They offer love and moral support and prayers in behalf of those who have taken their place.

Even those who can no longer do anything for themselves, are still the reason why their caregivers do countless acts of love that would forever have been left undone.

These are the routine callings of which the world is full. Now let's discuss those SPECIAL callings called Vocations, spelled with a capital V, that are offered to, or at least accepted by, very few.

Why is it, do you think, that there is such a shortage of persons willing to devote their lives to the highest callings? I think there are three main reasons.

The first is that we want too many benefits without burdens. For example, recently a friend of mine, who has three sons, complained to me about the shortage of priests. She said, "Why don't they send us more priests?" I asked her, "Who are THEY? And why not send us one of your boys?" The thought that she might have a sacrifice to make amused her. She laughed at me.

The second reason is that in our day and age, almost no one seems willing to make a lifelong commitment any more. As one lady told me, "I don't want to get married by a priest because it would be too hard to get out of it." It has even been suggested that one should change professions every ten years. Yet there are those callings, like Marriage and the Priesthood and Religious Life, which take a lifetime to plan and execute.

The third reason is that we are conditioned by the ever popular "Don't blame me" mentality, which excuses wrongdoing by calling it an illness or by blaming it on someone else. For example, people who set fires or loot stores in a riot are not criminals anymore, but victims of "Mob Frenzy'"or "Rage Syndrome." Children who kill their parents are afflicted with "Chronic Abuse Syndrome." A man who was fired from his job because he was always late for work claimed to be suffering from "Chronic Tardiness Syndrome." It was suggested that a good remedy for his ridiculous ailment would simply be "Get out of bed!"

So I would say that what we need is, first, the willingness to make sacrifices for things worth having, and second, to have the courage to keep all our commitments, and third, to accept responsibility for all our actions.

Let me add one more important consideration about Vocations, namely, that even the highest Vocation is only an invitation, which the individual is free to accept or to decline. A person who says, "No, I'd rather do something else," is still pleasing to God. But wouldn't you agree that the willingness to say yes to a challenging calling when one is free to say no is one of the most attractive features of my vocation?

A calling, especially an unusual one, is not always clear. When I was young, I could not have imagined my life turning out the way it did. Now, looking back, I can see how each coincidence was only a part of God's plan for me.

Perhaps God has chosen you for a very special place in his Providence. Don't be afraid to accept the challenge. If God calls you, he will provide the means. Whatever your calling turns out to be, strive to be the best you can be.

We commit ourselves generously, we carry out our commitments faithfully, we accept our responsibilities fully and finally, we back up one another with our prayers.

Perhaps you would like to include in your daily prayers a prayer for Vocations like this:

O Father, please help us all to find our place in your providence for our day. Especially give the young and the undecided the wisdom and strength to say yes to their call. May love be always our first and finest motivation. In Jesus' Name we pray. Amen.

JESUS AND HIS YOKE

The Jews, whom Jesus invited to come to him with their burdens and weariness, were people living under endless rules and restrictions of Jewish law that put heavy burdens on them and made their efforts to serve God difficult and exhausting. They were under a yoke of submission, because of the pickiness of the Scribes and Pharisees.

Jesus also put his followers under a yoke, but he promises that his yoke will be easy. The Greek word that we translate "easy" has the meaning of "well fitting." "My yoke is well fitting and my burden light," he says.

In Jesus' day, ox yokes were handmade to fit the individual ox. The ox would first come to be measured just as you might be measured for tailor-made clothes. After measuring the ox, the yoke maker would carve out a rough version of the yoke from a piece of wood. When it was ready, the ox would be brought in for alterations. A well-fitted yoke would make it possible for the slow and bulky animal to pull a plow or ox cart comfortably.

Jesus and his yoke were especially impressed on me by a young mother I once visited in the hospital. She told me that she had a little boy who was severely retarded and that she would never be able to have another child. Far from being bitter, she felt that God had specially chosen her for the challenge of loving and caring for her special child. In fact, she felt enriched by her special calling. She felt that it was as though God was saying to her, "I know you can handle it." She did it out of love.

And once there was a man who became very frustrated with his job because whenever he tried to do his work, he met with constant delays and interruptions and complications. But he had a great love for those who needed him. He finally came to the conclusion that his special yoke consisted of the patient endurance of frustration and this brought him peace of mind. His love-inspired faithfulness to his commitment made all the difference.

Another example is this: I often marvel at the cheerful ways the girls in the front office here do their work. When they are trying to finish stacks of urgent paperwork they are constantly interrupted by callers at the desk and on the phone. It is hard to believe that they ever get their work done and that they can keep it up for years on end without going stark raving mad. They don't do it just for the pay.

Examples such as these show how important a part our attitude can play in our lives. Attitude is more important than whether we succeed or we fail, than what others say or think of us, than whether we are rewarded or ignored. It would seem that accomplishment consists of 10% facts and 90% what we do with them.

"Come to me and I will refresh you. My yoke is easy and my burden light," said Jesus.

The thought of putting yokes around our necks has its humorous side, but at the same time, it is rich in its meaning.

Consider that when Jesus places a yoke on our shoulders, it will fit well because when he asks anything of us, it will never be too much for us to bear. If it is, he will also give us the strength we need.

The thing that makes our burden light is love. A heavy burden given and carried with love is not so burdensome any more.

We first took Jesus' yoke on our shoulders in infancy when we were Baptized into union with him and we were washed clean of Adam's sin. We became adopted children of our Heavenly Father and living temples of the Holy Spirit. Now, as Jesus' followers, we must put into practice his Great Commandment of love: "Love one another as I have loved you."

Thoughts such as these in the midst of struggle can be a source of refreshment and encouragement because they remind us that our burdens are a privileged sharing in the burdens that the Lord Jesus chose to bear for us. His cross led to his Glorification and so will ours.

So, what if our life is so short and so uncertain? What if we exist on a speck of a planet spinning in a vast universe? What if our best efforts so often fail?

Our great purpose this side of heaven is to strive to make love always be our first and finest motivation—to wear Jesus' yoke with gratitude and appreciation—to be the most dependable of all people.

Many a time in the hospital the mother of a newborn baby has summed up her feelings by saying, "It was hard but it was worth it."

Whenever you feel weary and find life burdensome say, "Jesus, I love you."

You will be better for it.

These few examples of his writings and homilies give us insight into Fr. Kram's love of God and neighbor.

CHAPTER THIRTEEN

Prayers

In praying, do not babble like the pagans, who think that they will be heard because of their many words. Do not be like them. Your Father knows what you need before you ask him. This is how you are to pray:

> *"Our Father in heaven, hallowed be your name,*
>
> *Your kingdom come, your will be done,*
>
> *On earth as in heaven.*
>
> *Give us today our daily bread,*
>
> *And forgive us our debts,*
>
> *As we forgive our debtors;*
>
> *And do not subject us to the final test,*
>
> *But deliver us from the evil one."*

If you forgive others their transgressions, your heavenly Father will forgive you. But if you do not forgive others, neither will your Father forgive your transgressions. (Matthew 6:7–15)

Father Charles believed strongly in the power of prayer. Praying was an important part of his life.

Here is an interesting writing of his titled "Unceasing Prayer."

Life is full of uncertainty. We attend a party one day and a funeral the next. We smile and then we cry. In the course of a lifetime, we must all go through many a storm. Like Peter sinking in the waves, we can often say our best prayers in times of stress, but what a narrow attitude it would be if we were to limit our prayers only to times of trouble. We must learn to pray every day and in many ways.

A man once asked his pastor, "Father, is it okay to smoke while praying?" The priest said, "Absolutely not!" And he scolded the man for his irreverence. So the man asked another priest, but this time he rephrased the question, "Father, is it okay to pray while smoking?" This time the answer was, "Certainly, I do it all the time."

A lady once told me that she prays five rosaries every day and another woman showed me a stack of worn prayer cards from which she read prayers every day.

Can we pray too much? A better question would be, how many and what kind of prayers would we say well and without neglecting our duties? A housewife and mother, for example, must not neglect the children for the sake of more time to pray.

One way to solve such a prayer problem is to offer our whole day to God in the morning by what is commonly called a "Morning Offering," such as, "Lord, I offer you everything I do today for" and then mention the things for which you especially want to pray. Thus your whole day becomes a prayer.

Another way many devout persons find useful is to light a candle. On a birthday cake the candles say, "Happy Birthday to you, happy birthday to you; may you have many more." In a religious setting, a burning candle says, "Lord, as I go my way, my candle stands in my place as a symbol of my prayer rising up to you."

Or, let's take another example. Every now and then, when I come down to the chapel at night, I would see an elderly man silently sitting in one of the pews. He did not seem to be saying anything. He was engaged in a form of wordless prayer known as contemplation, which consists of simply being in God's presence, waiting and listening, enjoying God's company.

Finally, we should put in a word for the Novena, a nine-day prayer. Keeping up a prayer for some special intention for any length of time is well in keeping with the teaching of the Scriptures to be persistent, and not give up if the answer is slow coming. Use a Novena card of your choice or make up a Novena prayer in your own words if you like.

God is unpredictable and we do not know how he will answer our prayers or where he will lead us next. Sometimes he grasps us by the hand and rescues us as Jesus did Peter. Sometimes he works in the background and answers us in an unexpected way and sometimes only after a long delay.

There is evidence throughout Fr. Charles's writings that he was deeply devoted to a life of prayer. Many of the prayers he used were the traditional prayers of the Church, such as the Prayer Before a Crucifix, the Litany of Loreto, the Act of Consecration to the Sacred Heart of Jesus, the Prayer to St. Michael the Archangel, the Prayer to St. Jude, the Litany of the Sacred Heart of Jesus, the Miraculous Invocation to St. Therese, the Hail Mary, the Peace Prayer of St. Francis of Assisi, the Lord's Prayer, the Glory Be, etc.

There were also beautiful expressions of love that he apparently composed that were found among his papers. Several examples are very touching:

PRAYER TO MARY

Ever glorious and blessed Mary, Queen of Virgins, Mother of Mercy, hope and comfort of all dejected and desolate souls, through that sword of sorrow, which pierced thy tender heart whilst thine only Son, Christ Jesus, Our Lord, suffered death and ignominy on the cross; through that filial tenderness and pure love he had for thee, grieving in thy grief, whilst from his cross he recommended thee to the care and protection of his disciple St. John:

Take pity, I beseech thee, on my poverty and necessities; have compassion on my anxieties and cares; assist and comfort me in all my infirmities and miseries, of what kind so ever. Thou art the mother of mercies, the sweet consolatrix and only refuge of the needy and the orphan, of the desolate and afflicted. Cast therefore an eye of pity on a miserable, forlorn child of Eve, and hear my prayer.

For since, in just punishment of my sins, I find myself encompassed by a multitude of evils, and oppressed with much anguish of spirit, whither can I fly for more secure shelter, O Mother of My Lord and Savior Jesus Christ, than under the wings of thy maternal protection? Attend then, I beseech thee, with an ear of pity and compassion, to my most humble and earnest request.

I ask it through the infinite mercy of thy dear Son; through that love and condescension wherewith he embraced our nature, when, in compliance with the Divine Will, thou gave thy consent, and whom, after the expiration of nine months, thou didst bring forth from the chaste enclosure of thy womb our Lord who came to visit this world and bless it with his presence. I ask it through that anguish of mind wherewith thy beloved Son, our dear Savior, was overwhelmed on Mount Olivet when he besought his eternal Father to remove from him, if possible, the bitter chalice of his future passion.

I ask it through the three-fold repetition of his prayers in the garden, from whence afterwards, with dolorous steps and mournful tears, thou didst accompany him to the doleful theater of his death and sufferings. I ask it through the weals and sores of his virginal flesh, occasioned by the cords wherewith he was bound and by the whips wherewith he was scourged. I ask it through the scoffs and ignominies by which he was insulted; through the false accusations and unjust sentence by which he was condemned to death, and which he bore with heavenly patience.

I ask it through his bitter tears and bloody sweat; through his silence and resignation, his sadness and grief of heart. I ask it through the blood, which trickled from his sacred head when struck with a reed and pierced with the crown of thorns. I ask it through the excruciating torments he suffered, when his hands and feet were fastened with gross nails to the tree of the cross. I ask it through his vehement thirst, and the bitter potion of vinegar and gall. I ask it through his dereliction on the cross, when he exclaimed, "My God, My God, why hast Thou forsaken me?" I ask it through his mercy extended to the good thief, and through his recommending his precious soul and spirit into the hands of his eternal Father before he expired, saying, "All is consummated."

I ask it through the blood mixed with water, which issued from his sacred side when pierced with a lance, and whence a flood of grace and mercy has flowed to us. I ask it through his immaculate life, his bitter passion, and ignominious death on the cross, at which nature itself was thrown into convulsions, by the bursting of rocks, the rending of the veil of the Temple, the earthquake, and the darkness of the sun and moon. I ask it through his descent into hell, where he comforted the saints of the old law with his presence and led captivity captive.

I ask it through his glorious victory over death, when he arose again to life, and through the joy which his appearance for forty days after gave thee, his blessed mother, his apostles and disciples, and when in their presence he miraculously ascended into heaven. I ask it through the grace of the Holy Spirit, infused into the hearts of his disciples, when he descended upon them in the form of fiery tongues, and by which they were inspired with zeal in the conversion of the world, when they went to preach the Gospel.

I ask it through the awful appearance of thy son at the last dreadful day, when he shall come to judge the living and the dead. I ask it through the compassion he bore thee in this life, and the ineffable joy thou didst feel at thine assumption into heaven, where thou art eternally absorbed in the sweet contemplation of his Divine perfections. O glorious and ever blessed Virgin, comfort the heart of thy supplicant, by obtaining for me _____ and as I am persuaded by my Divine Savior who honors thee as his beloved mother, to whom he refuses nothing, because thou asks for nothing contrary to his honor, so let me speedily experience the efficacy of thy powerful intercession, according to the tenderness of thy maternal affection, and his filial loving heart, who mercifully grants the requests and complies with the desires of those that love and fear him.

Wherefore, O Most Blessed Virgin, besides the object of my present petition, and whatever else I may stand in need of, obtain for me also of thy dear Son, Our Lord and Our God, a lively faith, firm hope, perfect charity, true contrition of heart, unfeigned tears of compunction, sincere confession, condign satisfaction, abstinence from sin, love of God and my neighbor, contempt of the world, patience to suffer affronts and ignominies, nay even, if necessary, an opprobrious death itself, for love of thy Son, our Savior Jesus Christ.

Obtain likewise for me, O sacred Mother of God, perseverance in all good works, performance of good resolutions, mortification of self-will, a pious conversation through life, and, at my last moments, a strong and sincere repentance, accompanied by such a lively, attentive presence of mind, as may enable me to receive the last sacraments of the Church worthily, and die in thy friendship and favor.

Lastly, obtain through thy Son, I beseech thee, for the souls of my parents, brethren, relatives, and benefactors, both living and dead, life everlasting from the only giver of each good and perfect gift, the Lord God Almighty: to whom be all power, now and forever. Amen.

PRAYER FOR CLERGY

Let us pray for:

The Holy Father—Fill him with your grace, Lord.

Cardinals, archbishops, and bishops—Give them your gifts, Lord.

Diocesan priests—Never leave them, Lord.

Priests in seminary work—Give them your wisdom, Lord.

Priests in hospital work—Give them constancy, Lord.

Priests who are ill—Give them good health, Lord.

Priests in danger—Deliver them, Lord.

Priests who are weak—Strengthen them, Lord.

Priests who are poor—Relieve them, Lord.

Priests who are zealous—Help them, Lord.

Priests who want to love you—Enkindle their hearts, Lord.

Priests who are sad—Console them, Lord.

Priests who are worried—Give them peace, Lord.

Priests who are old—Sustain them, Lord.

Priests who are young—Impel them for your glory, Lord.

Priests who are alone—Accompany them, Lord.

Missionary priests—Protect them, Lord.

Priests who are teachers—Enlighten them, Lord.

Priests who direct souls—Instruct them, Lord.

Parish priests—Give them prudence, Lord.

Religious priests—Make them perfect, Lord.

Priests and religious who have died—Bring them to glory, Lord.

On all the Church, militant and suffering—Lord, have mercy.

FOR ALL PRIESTS

Give them your wisdom, Lord.

Give them virtues.

Give them patience and charity.

Give them obedience and kindness.

Give them a burning zeal for souls.

Give them an intense love for the Eucharist.

Give them loyalty to the Holy See and to their bishops.

Give them respect for their dignity.

Give them a great love for Mary.

Give them rectitude and justice.

Give them the gift of counsel.

Give them strength in their labors.

Give them peace in their sufferings.

Give them humility and generosity.

Let them be the light of souls.

Let them be the salt of the earth.

Let them practice sacrifice and self-denial.

Let them enkindle hearts with the love of Mary.

Let them be other Christs.

Let them be holy in body and soul.

May they be men of prayer.

May faith shine forth in them.

May they be concerned only for the salvation of souls.

May they be faithful to their priestly vocation.

May their hands know only how to bless.

May they burn with love for you and Mary.

May all their steps be for the glory of God.

May the Holy Spirit possess them and give them his gifts and fruits in abundance.

LET US PRAY.

O God, Father, Son, and Holy Spirit, you are the soul and the life of the Church. Hear the prayers we offer for priests. We ask this through the Immaculate Heart of Mary, their protector and guide. Amen.

Here is another fine prayer of Fr. Kram:

PRAYER FOR VOCATIONS

Lord, please help us all to find our place in your providence for our day.

Especially give the young and the undecided the wisdom and strength to say "Yes" to your call.

May love be always our first and finest motivation.

We ask this in Jesus' name. Amen.

As Fr. Charles struggled with the powerful adversary called cancer, he wrote some of his most profound prayerful thoughts. He uttered without restraint what was in his heart and mind and soul to Almighty God in several prayers. Here is one of the most touching and inspiring examples of love of God (read it slowly and carefully):

PRAYER ABOUT HEALING

Let me begin by re-dedicating myself to my life's purpose, whatever it may be. Lord, let me tell you how I feel about how my life is going now. I intend to be your faithful servant in every way you want of me as long as I live.

I see the things that are happening to me as being your Holy Will and I have no complaints whatever about it. Whatever will happen will happen as you continue to provide for me. I am happy to know that I am well thought of by so many.

As for my physical condition, my intention is that there is no form of medical treatment or surgery for me. I will thrive without it.

I have no intention of lapsing into depression or despair or lack of motivation or fear of death. I do not pray to plead or bargain with you for a cure, for I have nothing to give you in return. I cannot fight cancer in any of the ways that doctors recommend, but I renew my commitment and gratitude to you, convinced that your will is being done, no matter what.

I have no specific plan for the eradication of cancer, but I live by my prayerful and prayer-like attitude of devotion and acceptance. I do not know just where you are leading me, so I do not have a robust, aggressive prayer for a specific outcome, including eradication of the cancer itself.

It will regress spontaneously, as all my favorite formulae are abandoned. I have no program designed to banish cancer but I will simply be myself. I honor the experiences that emerge from the innermost depths of my heart. I will not follow any specific formula to rid myself of cancer.

My healing will not be from the outside, as though my spirituality were a commodity or a drug, but it will emerge from the center of my being, where you live. The key to my regression is in simply being true to myself and to you. I go beyond all formulae, paths, programs, or ulterior wishes, including perhaps even the hope that the cancer will disappear. I trust with all my heart that you, my Father, are pleased with me.

Grant that I may never lapse into depression or despair or lack of motivation or fear of death, but that I may remain always true to myself and grateful and committed to your will, wherever you may want to lead me.

I have decided to get well. I am not a statistic. I direct my body to abide by the following instructions: I direct that whatever cells or powers or forces in my body that remove swelling, pain, stiffness, irritation, or abnormal growth to get on the move and to keep moving, surging through the spots that need attention, so that soon my ailments will come under control. I direct my body to make and send forth huge numbers of red cells to bring my red cell count back up to normal. I direct my body to make full supplies of the white cells that kill cancer and infection. I direct my body also to mobilize all the forces that I need for healing and to put them into action.

I see my body accepting my request and responding vigorously. I see my will and its great power to heal, making me well and strong again. I see swarms of my tiny piranha fish nibbling away at any tumors or neoplasm, until they have nibbled down to the healthy tissue, leaving the area smooth and clean. I see the areas growing fresh new healthy tissue where the abnormal growths had been. I see a wonderful blue-green wave of healing washing down through my body from head to toe. I see my disposition full of optimism and enthusiasm. I dissolve all hopelessness, fear, doubt, despair, or lack of motivation. I see myself fulfilling God's will to the fullest.

I see myself as having no objection whatever to what God wants of me. I see my trials and troubles bringing me closer and closer to my Dear Savior, cross and all. I see my love for him growing ever more intense with each trial. As my burdens grow heavier, I love him more and more. I see myself being cleansed more and more from the debris that may be cluttering my soul and making me unworthy of him. I see myself preparing more and more for that joyful day of the Resurrection when the Lord Jesus returns to take me home.

This quote from St. Josemaria Escriva hits the nail on the head: "You don't know how to pray? Put yourself in the presence of God, and as soon as you have said, 'God, I don't know how to pray!' you can be sure you have already begun."

In all times of prayer, remember that the most important part of praying is quietly listening to God as he communicates to you.

CHAPTER FOURTEEN

In Death Do We Part

O merciful Jesus, stretched on the cross, be mindful of the hour of my death.
O most merciful Sacred Heart of Jesus, opened with a lance, shelter me at
the last moment of my life. O Blood and Water, which gushed forth from the
Heart of Jesus, be a fountain of unfathomable mercy for me at the hour of
my death. O dying Jesus, Hostage of mercy, avert the Divine wrath at the
hour of my death. (Diary of Divine Mercy, 813)

O my Jesus, may the last days of my exile be spent totally according to your
holy will. I unite my sufferings, my bitterness, and my last agony itself to
your Sacred Passion, and I offer myself for the whole world to obtain an
abundance of God's mercy for souls. . . . I firmly trust and commit myself
entirely to your will, which is mercy itself. Your mercy will be everything for
me at the last hour. (Diary of Divine Mercy, 1574)

These two prayers were part of Fr. Kram's collection of important prayers, prayers that were very significant in his life. They
were taken from the Diary of St. Faustina Kowalska, the Polish nun
who was devoted to the message of Divine Mercy. Her visions of
and communications with Jesus, which she recorded in her diary,
form the basis for her canonization and our devotion known as the
Divine Mercy Apostolate. Her communications with Jesus began

on February 22, 1931. She died on October 5, 1958, when she was only thirty-three years old.

Father Charles did not dwell on the thought of dying, but he did have a solid grasp of what it entailed. His experiences in the hospital where life and death were sometimes held in a delicate balance helped form his attitude toward death. Here is an article he wrote for the people of the Diocese of Victoria as found in *The Catholic Lighthouse*, the official publication of the diocese:

Life—Where Will It End?

To be or not to be; that is the question. It comes from Shakespeare and is a very good question because the drive to stay alive is the strongest instinct in our nature. It is said, for example, that persons who attempt suicide usually do not want to die but want to be reached in time. Every now and then we hear of some desperate person calling a friend and saying, "I just took a handful of pills; get me to the hospital quick."

It is also said that even the lost souls in hell, in spite of their torments and great sense of loss and their utter despair, prefer not to have their existence extinguished.

We hold onto life for dear life but we are all destined one day to die. Every generation in history has died out completely. On the day we are born, we already begin to die. In fact, the most final, and unavoidable, and usually the most unwelcome fact of life is death.

Every day in the hospital, we see the fight to improve and preserve and prolong life. Money saved up during a whole lifetime of labor is spent to buy just a little more time in this life.

Even when death finally comes, our bodies are made to look as though we were still alive.

Now, instead of dwelling on thoughts on death to the point of becoming morbid, let us consider life after death, or if you will, the afterlife.

We pray that the dead may rest in peace, but not in the same sense in which we wish a friend a good night's sleep. The souls of the dead are very much alive and aware.

They no longer have eyes to see with or ears to hear with or any other senses to collect information with, but freed from the limitations of the body, they can now truly begin to live. The mind is unhindered in its thinking and the will is unhindered in its loving.

In seeing God face to face, the soul is in ecstasy and needs to search no more. There is only the pure and intense activity of knowing and loving. No more fear or doubt or struggling, only joy and peace and security—eternal rest.

Now, back to earth. How old are you? What do you suppose is the average age in your town today? We all hope one day to live with God in an eternal "now," but for the present we are like the little flowers that spring up so fresh and colorful in the morning but by twilight are already fading away.

So, where will each of us be a hundred years from now or even fifty years from now? Perhaps, fifty years from now, some of us will still be alive, old and gray. Many of us will be in our graves.

Wouldn't we all like to stay young and vigorous as long as possible? And as we grow older, don't we have some wonderful memories stored up? But is it not also true that our memories are deceptive? They bring back too many happy events and too few sad, and leave us very restless, wishing for those carefree days that actually never existed. But the past is gone, never to return, and the future is not yet here. All we have is the present moment.

The only thing to do, then, is to spend our lives wisely, one day at a time.

May I suggest that you make it a daily practice to make a morning offering, offering to Christ all that you will do that day? Every prayer, work, joy, and suffering will then become a precious gift to him. I always offer mine for special intentions such as to thank him for favors received or as reparation for my sins or to ask him for help with my needs.

And during the day, why not offer individual acts to him by saying, "This is for you, Jesus; I love you"? Doing everything for the love of Christ does so much to make even our sorrows and frustrations and failures worthwhile.

How consoling it is to consider that as our outer grace and beauty fade with the passing years, our inner beauty can still grow little by little as we become more and more like him in whose image we are made, and that after the last beat of our heart, when the body can no longer support life, it will be laid aside for a little while to await the Resurrection.

How glorious it will be on the last day "when Christ will raise our mortal bodies and make them like his own in glory" (taken from the Mass, Eucharistic Prayer III).

In a way, after the Resurrection, we will be better off than the angels. We will again be body and spirit and they will still be only spirit.

Now, a final question: "Why did God choose to make *us* rather than the same number of others from all the millions of possible people who will never exist?" Only God knows why he so favored us.

We live in a world in which we all depend on one another, and where the actions and omissions of each of us help or hinder the rest of us, so among us there is a time and a place for each of us to live and to die. May God help us from day to day to find it.

As we move on to our death and to our life with God, let us place all our trust in him, and let us be of good cheer. God will provide.

Lord Jesus, thank you for bringing our minds and hearts always back to thoughts of you. Help us, by the death you freely accepted, to find the strength to live and die for you. Grant that "by your cross and Resurrection, we may be set free, for you are the Savior of the world" (taken from the Mass, Fourth Memorial Acclamation). Amen.

Another writing of Fr. Kram's titled "Wisdom and Death" expresses timely thoughts on everyday life that are beneficial to all of us.

In the last few weeks many new babies have made their arrival here. We all begin life with a mind like a blank slate on which we record new experiences every day. In the beginning, babies are tyrants. They cause disturbances any time of the day or night, whenever they are cold or hungry or wet. They demand instant results *now*.

But over the years we live and learn. We see better and better how things fit together, how one thing leads to another. We learn the meaning of sacrifice. We learn the value of waiting, and the satisfaction of working toward a goal. In addition to the lessons we learn from our experiences, we are surrounded with reminders of the course our nature takes. Even the buds of spring growing to maturity, and then to the harvest time, followed by falling leaves and the dead of winter keep reminding us of our own mortality.

As the baby becomes a youth and then an adult and then faces old age, each stage of life brings one closer to the day when we must depart from this world and leave everything behind.

We might say that the most obvious fact of life is death. Naturally speaking, death is so useless and absurd. It ends our earthly existence and frustrates all our plans.

But for the Christian, death is the harvest time, the fulfillment of the reason for which God made him, the completion of everything he has struggled for.

The wisdom that we each acquire through our lifetime of experience, and through what has been revealed to us through the Lord Jesus, makes it impossible for us to see death as a sad and unavoidable necessity, but rather, as the gateway to our complete acceptance of God and our own final fulfillment.

In the face of all these facts of life and of death, today would be a fine day to resolve to make sure that you are always ready for death, and to remove as soon as possible any obstacle that might make your death a thing to fear.

Let every new baby, every aged person, every falling leaf be a precious reminder to be always alert and ready, with lamp lit, for the bridegroom's coming.

Lord Jesus, thank you for your timely warning about those things that are supremely important to us.

In the Liturgy for the thirty-third Sunday in Ordinary Time (Cycle A), the Gospel reading from Matthew 25:14–30 included Jesus' parable of the Faithful Servant, and Fr. Charles gave an interesting homily entitled "Fulfilling Our Commitments" in which he made these astute observations:

We think of death as the end of life. Death is not the end but is the beginning of a new kind of life. One author has compared death to the birth of a baby. In its mother's womb, the baby is content and secure. It is never hungry or thirsty or cold. The only sound it hears is the beating of its mother's heart. It is in a happy place from which it would wish never to leave.

But then comes the baby's time to be born. It is suddenly pushed out into a strange and exciting new world where there are bright lights and music, soft voices and laughter and loving embraces. The baby then says to himself, "I had no idea all this was waiting for me. I sure wouldn't want to ever have to go back to that dark and dull old place from which I came."

If we could experience for just a brief moment what heaven is like, we would all be most eager to go there and leave this world behind.

So, should we be afraid to die? The virtue of hope gives us the firm assurance that God will give us everything we need to be saved and, in the end, salvation itself. A healthy fear of death prompts us to trust God as though everything depended on him and to work as though everything depended on us.

No truer words were ever spoken.

We have seen throughout this journey through the life of Fr. Charles Kram that, while he did not dwell on the thought of death, he did stay prepared for it and tried to help everyone around him to make their preparations.

We now turn our attention to the end of his earthly life.

The story of how many obstacles in life he faced is a story of courage and of love of God and neighbor and of service to humanity and, above all else, of humility in its highest degree. In the final months, weeks, days, and then hours of his life, these beautiful qualities of humanity shine even more brightly.

It was in the spring of 1999 that the doctor diagnosed Fr. Charles's new pains to be the result of a malignant tumor on his left kidney. The shock of hearing your doctor tell you "It is cancer" can be unnerving no matter how gently or politely or professionally the revelation is phrased. Cancer is cancer, and there is no way to sugarcoat the news.

Father Charles was a man of great faith in God and of God's purpose for him in this life. This strong faith played a large part in his consideration of how to proceed.

The doctor's early recommendation was that Fr. Charles seek the medical advice of the staff at M. D. Anderson Hospital in Houston. This was sound advice, and Fr. Charles gave due consideration to that idea. Weighing very heavily in his consideration was his strong and complete confidence in his physician, Dr. Crayton Ciborowski, whom he respected beyond a doubt.

Yet was this God's will? What was God's desire for him? Recall-ing the many instances in Scripture when Jesus readily cured all manner of afflictions and every form of disability presented to him, it certainly appeared likely that God could cure his cancer if that was what God willed. And there was the answer.

Father Charles simply prayed that God's will be done. We read his deeply moving prayer in the last chapter.

Father Charles chose to let the medical procedures for his care and comfort be carried out without any heroic efforts to save his life. Complying with the will of God was more important to him than any other consideration.

And so it was. The doctors and hospital staff went about their work to care for his comfort and he, Fr. Charles Kram, went about his ministry to all God's children with whom he came into contact.

God provides for our needs. All we need to do is respond with love for all humanity. Father Charles set himself more completely on that course.

Janet Pohl, from whom we heard earlier about Fr. Charles's hos-pital ministry, remembered this time of Father's life in this manner:

> I remember the day Father told me that he had a tumor on his kidney. He said he needed to have surgery to have it removed, but would have to go to Houston to have it done. He said he really didn't want to go, but his doctor wanted him to do it. I told him that it was his decision and that we would pray for a miracle. Father decided not to pursue the surgery but to live out his life in God's hands. He con-tinued his life at the hospital, giving to others as much as he could. Father was very prepared for his journey home.
>
> He organized everything down to what he would wear to where things needed to be returned, and how his posses-sions needed to be distributed. I remember a day about a couple of weeks before he died, Father was still in bed as he seemed to be more and more as his illness progressed, and he requested that I come to his room. I usually assisted him with things he needed.

Father instructed me that the respirator he was using at the time was a loaner. He told me where the box was kept for when it would be time to return it. At that time I didn't realize it but Father was making sure things were organized for when he would die. He never actually told me this was the reason, but that he was making sure things were in place.

The day I received the call that Father was dying, my sister and I drove to the hospital to join several other co-workers and friends gathered around Father's bed. We were saying the rosary with the bishop when Father took his last breath.

Father asked very little of other people and when he did, it was always "when you have time." He never demanded anything, especially the care he received upon which he was totally dependent. Father was always patient and never complained even when people grew impatient with him.

I will always miss Father's Masses which were so inspirational and ended with a joke he had heard somewhere. The sound of his wheelchair will no longer be heard coming down the hall or around the next corner. He is no longer with us in body, but will always remain in our hearts. When I pass by his picture in the hall just outside the chapel, I can still feel the love in his eyes as though he is still watching over us. I still talk to him when things get tough and I need a little pick-me-up.

Father was my rock and still is when I think I can't cope or deal with things in my life. At times like these, I remember how strong he was and that he never complained and that's what helps me through life's many challenges to this very day.

As the debilitating effects of the cancer heaped on top of the breathing problems and the paralysis from the polio all together laid claim to his quality of life, Fr. Charles spent more and more time in bed and away from his devoted ministry to the sick.

The "straw that broke the camel's back" in his struggle for life occurred on July 30, 2000, when Fr. Charles somehow slid out of the end of his rocking bed as the front end tipped downward. As he slid to the floor, the blow to his fragile frame was too much. His left hip bone was fractured in such a way that repair was not possible. There was nothing more to do but to try to make him comfortable.

Anne Marie Germani, a dear and devoted friend of Fr. Charles, related for us her last visit with him:

The last day I spent with him was the day before he died. He smiled in his sufferings and spoke of all the days when we worked together. He had trouble breathing that day, yet he only cared for those who were with him. He smiled in his pain. He was resigned to soon be leaving us. He was at peace with the knowledge that he would soon be with the Lord, yet he still lived to be of service. Facing death, he prayed, "Not my will but Christ's will be done."

Christ exhibited, in Fr. Kram, the perfection of his priestly character in all its loftiness and in all its lowliness—its loftiness in his unshakable consciousness of his total consecration to God and its lowliness in his piercing consciousness of the frailty of human flesh that fears the cost of its own consecration.

He freely chose to divest himself of things and of self. He became the Lamb of God. He gave himself totally and unconditionally to the love of God. His vocation was love and love was his life. God walks among us every day, yet so many times we fail to recognize him in those closest to us. God called Fr. Kram. He gave himself back to God with every labored breath, with every heartbeat until his final "Amen." Pray for us, Reverend Father Charles.

Father Kram had chosen Benita Janecek Bordovsky to be the executor of his living will. Benita was also a life-long friend and she helped Father with many of his tasks, which included making his bank deposits, helping with his tax returns, and taking care of errands for him. Benita was with Father at the time of his death. She gave her reflection:

> Saturday morning, August 12, 2000, I helped at the St. Vincent Store, and visited my mother in the nursing home. I got home around 3 p.m. and planned to do some sewing. Suddenly, the realization came to me to go see Fr. Charles immediately.
>
> Upon arriving at the hospital, I found that Father was alone in his room. He did not respond to my greeting. I could tell something was seriously wrong. His eyes were closed, his stomach was distended and he was groaning with pain. I stayed with him to comfort him as best as I could.
>
> At 1:00 a.m. Sunday, August 13, he seemed to be getting progressively worse. I went to the nurses' station and inquired if the doctor had been notified of Father's condition. I was informed that he had been informed and that he ordered blood work. At 2 a.m. the doctor arrived and stayed until Father died. Pain medication was administered intravenously and the pain subsided. During the morning, hospital staff and friends and clergy came to pray and pay their respects. Bishop David Fellhauer and Fr. Gary Janak came and prayed. The bishop anointed Father and stayed with him until the end. I thank the Holy Spirit for allowing me to be with Fr. Charles in the moment of his passing into eternity.

Karen Roznovsky, who earlier gave a detailed recollection of Fr. Charles's hospital ministry, recalls details surrounding his death:

> I remember the Sunday morning that Fr. Kram died. My family and I had just gotten back home after Mass and my sister, Janet Pohl, received a phone call from Shari Fluitt, the Unit Secretary at the nurses' station. She was told that if we would like to see Fr. Kram one last time, we should hurry to the hospital as he was dying. Of course, we went.

Our group was Janet and her daughter, Krystal Pohl, and my daughter, Jenna Roznovsky, and I.

Doctor Ciborowski and a good many of Father's friends were there. My daughter Jenna, who was eleven years old then, recalls now that the room was full of people , people who truly loved Father. She says that she had the feeling that she was in God's presence in the room with such a peaceful and serene attitude among the people who were praying the rosary. The bishop arrived to also pray with us all. Before he arrived, though, those present were invited to speak to Fr. Charles to say our goodbyes.

Father will always be a part of the hospital's history and his impact was great. Although over the past thirteen years since he died, many of the employees and people he knew then have moved away or they died. But the stories are still told of this great man who worked amongst us in ministering to the patients and staff. He always thought we were taking care of him, but he was really taking care of us. His photo is on display in the hallway by the chapel and I always have to smile when I see him. Sometimes, when things aren't going so great, I take comfort in saying, "Father, help us!" It's just reassuring to know he is still with us in our hearts.

Father taught me to be grateful for the life I have. After all, if this man, with all his disabilities, could be positive and kind and so giving of himself to others, how can I not do likewise? He taught me to be grateful for the little things in life. He faced adversity and trials in his life but always overcame them by enjoying every moment of the day that he could. Though he suffered greatly, his is a story of hope, a story of acceptance, a story of making the best of one's circumstances. He had the ability to work through his disabilities through optimism, invention, and the drive to make himself as self-sufficient as possible while trying to not be a burden to others. He had an incredibly strong will and faith to fulfill his mission on earth to his greatest potential even under his present circumstances.

He took the talents God gave him and he multiplied them greatly.

"Father, into your hands, I commend my Spirit; and when he said that, he breathed his last" (Luke 23:46).

Father Charles William Kram, Jr., died August 13, 2000, at the age of seventy years, ten months, and thirteen days. Funeral arrangements were made in accordance with instructions he had filed with the Diocese of Victoria in Texas. Those instructions included a Rosary Service at St. Joseph Catholic Church in Yoakum on August 15 and the funeral Mass on Wednesday, August 16, at the same church with His Excellency, the Most Reverend David Fellhauer, bishop of the Diocese of Victoria in Texas officiating. Father Kram's instructions also requested that Deacon Paul Patek of Sts. Cyril and Methodius Church deliver the homily.

Deacon Patek offered these recollections for our reflection on Fr. Charles's life:

"Gladly will I glory in my infirmities." These words of St. Paul hung on a simple banner in the sanctuary of Sts. Cyril and Methodius Church in Shiner on December 5, 1975, on the ordination day of Fr. Charles Kram. Amid the pageantry of the day, these words echoed more loudly than the combined applause of the crowd and the harmonious voices of the choir. "Gladly will I glory in my infirmities" was a motto dear to the heart of Fr. Charles.

Father Charles was born September 30, 1929, in Shiner to Charles W. and Emma Zander Kram. He had one brother, Edgar, who preceded him in death, and one sister, Felicia Kram Argubright, who resides in Corpus Christi, and one sister who died at birth, and numerous nieces and nephews. Father Charles was baptized, confirmed, and ordained at Sts. Cyril and Methodius Church here in Shiner and graduated from St. Ludmila's Academy in 1946.

In September of 1946, he entered St. John's Seminary in San Antonio, Texas. Charles was ordained a Subdeacon in May of 1952. He never suspected it would be another twenty-three years before he would become a priest. On June 15, 1952, he contracted a severe case of polio, which disabled him and changed his plans completely.

Paralysis set in and he was rushed to the polio ward of the Robert B. Green Hospital in San Antonio to recuperate. After eight months, he was transferred to Gonzales Warm Springs for rehabilitation. There, he received a wheelchair, a lapboard, and pivoted arm supports, which enabled him to regain some use of his fingers. In the fall of 1953, he was discharged as a permanent quadriplegic.

Because of his condition, he was told he could no longer be ordained. A year and a half after the onset, he returned to his former home in Shiner where his parents cared for him. He was resigned not to allow his disappointment to dominate his thoughts.

He disliked the idea of self-pity, because it was a hindrance to his own development and was an embarrassment to others. He found his seminary training with emphasis on prayer to be a great help. He devoted much time to prayer and meditation.

The years passed by swiftly for him as he renewed his interest in HAM radio, reaching people in over 160 countries. He was an avid reader. He turned pages with the use of the same rubber-tipped stick held in his mouth that was required to operate his HAM radio equipment and an electric typewriter. He had a great sense of humor and enjoyed sharing jokes with everyone.

After twenty-three and a half years of patient efforts by his classmates and by the late Archbishops Robert Lucey and Francis Furey of San Antonio, the way was cleared for Charles Kram's ordination. He was overwhelmed with joy and happiness and, at the age of forty-six, he was ordained in a wheelchair on December 5, 1975.

His mother was already in the nursing home at the time, but he was still staying with his aged dad on the farm. His father ministered to his son faithfully for nearly a quarter of a century. In February of 1977, Fr. Kram's dad passed away and Charles's new home was at Huth Memorial Hospital, a forty-six-bed Catholic hospital here in Yoakum, where he ministered daily in his wheelchair chaplaincy.

He took his portable altar with him to celebrate daily Mass for the Sisters and occasional visitors. On Sunday, he preached a short homily and heard confessions. All the patients and all the staff members were drawn to him for he was such a ray of sunshine, someone to confide in, and moral support for many. We can all recall memories of him spending evenings seated near the nurses' station, reading, writing, and talking to people who got on and off the elevator.

Suffering a long illness is a vocation, a form of service. It is "redemptive" for it is a "direct sharing" of Christ. Only chosen souls are called to the ministry and apostolate of suffering and illness. If my eyes cannot see, then my hands and ears have to do the seeing for me. It is the same in the body of Christ.

In a pleasure-seeking society, when many people avoid pain at all costs, where drugs of all kinds are used to deaden the realities of life, then someone in the body must carry the cross for the rest of us. One such soul was Fr. Kram. The vocation of suffering is accomplished by the grace and strength to carry the cross, and the sufferer is redeemed and purified in the process.

At the conclusion of 1 Corinthians 13, St. Paul tells us there are three things in life that remain, three virtues central to our relationship with God. They never depreciate.

They never go out of style. They never perish. These three virtues are faith, hope, and love. The greatest heritage that anyone can leave is an abundant supply of these. Father Charles left us that kind of legacy. With St. Paul's words, we can outline the story of his life.

The first is "faith." With Fr. Charles, faith was more than a religious idea that prophets dream up to write Scripture. He lived it, as a necessity of life. He possessed a great faith in God, whose divine providence allowed him the cross he had to carry over the many years of his life. He had faith in his fellow man because he needed help, and depended on others for most things. And he had faith in himself, to overcome his disabilities or at least to be resigned to the situation.

It is written that if one has faith the size of a mustard seed, one can move mountains. As limited as he was, Fr. Charles climbed mountains and moved mountains, as he continued doing God's work, ministering to his people and accepting and embracing pain and suffering. He took his faith in God as a daily necessity, lifted it to its highest level, and applied it to all of his life. He left us a great legacy of faith.

The second word is "hope." In this regard, we can borrow the words of Job in the first reading, who himself carried a heavy burden of suffering. He says, "I know my redeemer lives, and that on the last day, he will stand upon the earth, then in my flesh, I shall see God."

Sometimes, the tendency during illness is to drift from optimism to despair, to move from bright hope to gray cynicism. Not so for our friend and colleague, Fr. Charles. The windows of his heart stayed open to the sunshine of the morning, letting in rays of hope to sustain him in his daily life. He left behind a "bountiful" legacy of hope.

The final word is "love." Not only is it the final word, it is the ultimate word. It is the highest virtue of which any human heart is capable. It is the greatest of all three. The New Testament tells us that all moral law can be summed up in one statement. "Love your neighbor as yourself." Think of it. All of man's ethical and moral responsibility is wrapped up in one simple word and that is LOVE.

When we reflect on the life of Fr. Charles, we can begin to understand how love was lived out in him in his gentleness, his kindness, his humor, and his warmth for people of all faiths. His love was "guidance" for the confused, "friendship" for the lonely, and "aid" for the poor in spirit.

If you have ever visited Yosemite Park in California, there are huge sequoia trees, which are part of God's magnificent creation. These trees stand out as giants, so majestically, for all to see. They are giant in stature, compared to the other trees of the forest.

For most of Fr. Charles's life, he was not able to stand, but in human stature, Fr. Kram stood tall. He was a giant of a man, a man of courageous, Christian timber by all his accomplishments, whose examples of faith, hope, and love stood tall for all to see.

It has often been said of Mother Teresa that she was a living saint. You know, I can't help but feel that within our own community, we also had a living saint in Fr. Charles Kram.

And so, our friend, Fr. Kram is gone. But we are richer for his having been here. He has left us a legacy of those things that matter most: faith, hope, and love.

This special man, called by God for a special mission in life, spoke to us even in the quietness of his daily living. Yes, God gave him a restricted life. Maybe God is asking the rest of us, whose handicaps are not so obvious, to begin to realize that man is not measured totally in the eyes of the Almighty God by intelligence, feats of endurance, or outstanding skills. This prophet, this saint, Fr. Charles, took life one day at a time. He not only spoke about love, he lived it to the fullest for the greater honor and glory of God.

Let us take comfort in the words of Jesus in the Gospel: "And this is the will of the one who sent me, that I should not lose anything of what God gave me." We believe with confidence that Fr. Charles has found life in all its fullness, found life in all beauty, joy, peace, and love, found life that is eternal and can never again be lost. For Jesus, who has come all the way from the kingdom of heaven from God's right hand has found Fr. Charles and brought him safely to his heavenly home. His death has been a peaceful and gentle passage into the arms of the welcoming and smiling Christ, who knows from his own personal experience what it is like to suffer. Yes, Fr. Kram is in safe keeping with Jesus.

The Christian who has suffered long and who has died in peace and with dignity has truly lived the Gospel. His funeral is a celebration of the power of the grace of God. It is a message for all of us of how to be truly human, of how to rise to the challenge of illness in ways that are both enriching and life giving, and above all, a proclamation that the human beings' real life is with God in eternal happiness.

"Gladly will I glory in my infirmities." May these words of St. Paul and the testimony of Fr. Charles Kram's life be an inspiration to us all to live the ways of Christ faithfully in our lives.

Thank you, God, for giving us Fr. Charles Kram.

Father Kram's remains were interred in Section C, Lot 17, Space 3, next to his parents' graves in the Shiner Catholic Cemetery in Texas.

May his soul and the souls of all the faithful departed, through the mercy of God, rest in peace. Amen.

CHAPTER FIFTEEN

Testimonials

Thus should one regard us: As servants of Christ and stewards of the mysteries of God. Now it is, of course, required of stewards that they be found trustworthy. (1 Corinthians 4:1–2)

When you reach out to friends and colleagues and acquaintances for their thoughts about someone, you must be prepared for the variety of responses you will receive.

The testimonials we received regarding Fr. Kram were varied, but positive. Even the two responders who felt he wasn't qualified for canonization praised his beautiful personal characteristics, such as his gentleness, fortitude, perseverance, sense of justice, dedication to helping the disadvantaged, and "old school" devotion to the established rules of life.

John Butschek met Fr. Charles when they were students at St. John's Seminary before John left the seminary for the life of a layman. Their friendship grew strong when Fr. Charles was the hospital chaplain and John was retired from his employment. John glows with admiration for Father's cheerfulness and positive attitude at all times in spite of his physical handicaps. Mr. Butschek observed that he didn't know St. Joseph personally, but he felt sure that Fr. Charles resembled St. Joseph by the way he lived his life to fulfill God's purpose for him. John went on to say that Fr. Charles had such complete trust in God that he had no fear of death. He told this story as an example:

Once when I was with him, his aspirator machine was not working properly. While he was telling me how to make adjustments, he was gasping for air. He showed no fear, only anxiety. He faced these kinds of incidents often in his life. Try to imagine your life depending on someone like me following your gasping instructions to adjust the machine properly and quickly.

John went on to say,

His speech and his sermons flow with a transparency impressive to all ages and education. He accepted his condition and purpose in life with the confidence and disposition that, if lived faithfully in God's honor and glory, his crown would await him in heaven in the eternal life with God.

Mary Butschek did a tremendous job of collecting and organizing Fr. Kram's writings and his homilies and the information on which much of his biography is based. She met Father in 1991 and found him to be a person of great strength and consolation. She offered these thoughts about him:

Just observing and being around and listening to Fr. Kram, I was struck by the fact that he seemed to embody the very virtues that I found most lacking in myself. After visiting Father, I came away spiritually renewed and determined to try to imitate him. If he could be as strong in his life as he was, it certainly encouraged me to try harder in my life and circumstances. In my opinion, Fr. Kram was the personification of humility and patience. He had absolutely no privacy. He was totally at the mercy of others to see about taking care of every bodily need he had, yet he accepted his situation with courage. He was very appreciative of even the smallest kindness shown to him. As a confessor, Fr. Kram had deep insights. Once I asked if he had the gift to read souls. He laughed and said he did not, but I always suspected that he did.

She went on to tell the story of a very troubling incident in her family that caused her considerable anguish that lasted many months. At one point Fr. Kram said he wished he could help her. Shortly thereafter, she said, the burden was lifted from her spirit. She told Father about her sudden relief and thanked him for whatever he did on her behalf; he just smiled and made some non-committal remark about being happy to be of service. She remained convinced that her burden was lifted through his intercession.

Mrs. Butschek offered these thoughts about his holiness:

> I think the universal church would be greatly blessed to declare Fr. Kram a saint. He would be the patron of the handicapped and a perfect example for them since he did so much for others when he himself was handicapped. Anyone who would be depressed or without hope could find inspiration in his life and the way he overcame so many difficulties while living a life of much holiness.

Sister M. Sylvia Grahmann, IWBS, knew Fr. Kram for twenty-nine years. Her assessment of his character is well-founded. We get these thoughts from her:

> Father Kram was always in a good mood. He had a sense of humor and never complained about how he felt. His gentleness radiated from him. He was patient, humble, and caring. He was never morose and he looked at the bright side of things. He was interested in what happened in school and in current events. There was no self-pity ever present in him.

> Since Father was a quadriplegic, he was unable to use his hands and feet. He spoke with a halting voice and constantly moved his head while he spoke. His body jerked as he spoke. Yet he was able to type by using a stick in his mouth. Although these motions made him a little less attractive, I admired his willingness to share and communicate with others.

Father was gentle, humble, kind, patient, long-suffering, meek, and always even-tempered. I never witnessed any mood swings. He was thankful and grateful for the priesthood. His submission to God's Will was touching. He reminded me of the suffering Christ. His faith was evident from the way he handled suffering. He waited almost twenty-five years to be ordained to the priesthood. Yet he never lost sight of his goal of becoming a priest. Anyone who can sit in a wheelchair day after day and always be in the same good mood must have great faith and trust in God. He was pleasant, jovial, and cheerful. A person who has all his personal needs attended to by other people must have deep faith and trust in God. His concern was always for others and not himself.

During his ministry at the hospital, Father was very diligent in preparing his homily for Sunday Mass. He typed with a stick in his mouth and it must have taken him hours to type his homilies.

Accepting his cross was a sign of humility. His meekness aided him in speaking kindly and gently with others.

She went on to say, "I definitely think Fr. Kram was a holy man. He was so much like Christ in the way he handled his suffering. I never met anyone with such patience and perseverance. In his hospital ministry, he worked tirelessly ministering to others even when you knew he himself was suffering greatly."

Phyllis Lauer was a friend for at least fifteen years. She met Father through his hospital chaplaincy and aided him with the eucharistic celebration. She made these observations about him:

Father Kram was a very good listener. He had a wonderful sense of humor. He was so patient and kind. He focused on others and not on himself and he had a way of making you feel important or special. What made him such a wonderful priest was the type of human being that he was. He was able to put himself "in your shoes." He understood so well your pain, your worries, your cares and pleasures, your joy and suffering. He related to others around him on such a personal level.

Father illuminated his faith daily and he trusted God wholeheartedly. He desired to be God's servant and he hoped for the kingdom of heaven. He had such a love for his fellow man. He expressed his faith, hope, and charity through his actions and his words.

Being a Hospital Chaplain put Fr. Kram in a position to perform the corporal works of mercy daily. He visited me several times when I was a patient in the hospital. He always expressed his concern for me with questions like these: "Are you hungry?"; "Do you need a blanket?"; "Are you thirsty?"; and "Is there someone to care for you at home?" He simply understood the needs and concerns of the patients and he tried to ease their suffering any way he could.

I always felt that Father loved everyone unconditionally, just as Jesus did and continues to do. He was the holiest person I ever met without him showing that holiness or flaunting it.

Sister Mary Lela (Anne Marie) Germani was the Director of Nursing at Huth Memorial Hospital when Fr. Charles arrived there in 1977. She knew him in her profession and then as a lay person after she left the religious community. They remained friends until his death. She remembers him fondly and respectfully and offered these recollections of him:

> I was the Director of Nursing responsible for the staff that cared for Fr. Kram after he came to Yoakum's Huth Memorial Hospital in 1977. As I recall, Fr. Halata was instrumental in Fr. Kram's coming to Yoakum after his father died and his mother was placed in the Shiner nursing home.
>
> Father C, as I called him, seemed a bit nervous initially, but soon the staff members at the hospital made him feel welcome. For his first birthday with us, September 30, 1977, we had a barbeque party for him. I think he might have

been overwhelmed that day because of the large number of staff and others who came to celebrate. His warmth and priestly exuberance touched everyone from the beginning when he first came to live with us. He made his way through the hospital on his electric wheelchair and the staff posted "stop signs" and "turn signs" in the hallways. This good will brought us all closer together.

He accepted his lifestyle without question and always with a smile, so unique to him, that made one want to smile in return. The beauty of his smile showed the very essence of his soul. He was careful with everyone, in that he always listened with eagerness to help in any way he could. There were days when he was ill, and yet his unique gift made everyone he touched feel as if they were his only concern.

I have never met a more compassionate human being. He truly cared for all those whose lives he touched. He had time for anyone who would ask him. Being confined to his wheelchair never made him a prisoner. He was ingenious in getting things done using his mouth stick. He was a Ham radio operator for years and he had his equipment brought to Huth Hospital when he came. He contacted people from around the world with his ministry.

Father Kram's communications also reached throughout the United States. He corresponded with grade school students in my twin sister Joanne's classes of over 230 students at St. Thomas More Catholic Grade School in Houston. He said how happy he was to have received the children's greetings and pictures. He loved every one of them and was encouraged to know that he had so many young friends praying for him.

His energy and enthusiasm were boundless. He always wanted to be a part of what was happening. As Hospital Chaplain he made daily rounds to all the patients. He was the chaplain for the Yoakum Fire Department as well, and Chief Hanna always made sure he took part in their monthly "boys' night" dinner-meetings. He took it upon himself to become a friend to whomever he met. Father C so well knew how to balance his physical problems with daily activities. His encouragement in the face of his own struggles was soul searching.

His handicap did not deter him from always being available. His freedom might have been hindered, but he had a wonderful spirit about not letting anything slow him down. His gentleness was readily seen when he would comfort those families who had lost a loved one. For those who were afraid, he had a kind word, which always gave the weakened spirit a lift. No matter how little the kindness, he always repaid it with his kind word and heart-warming smile.

His priesthood was evident from the moment he came to Yoakum. Nothing would deter his eagerness to be of assistance. He never stopped learning, especially helped by his new computer, where he prepared his homilies, and would practice them on me when he first started his ministry. Those were priceless hours of support and friendship.

His openness was so evident in trying just about anything! He loved to spend evenings in the park with the Sisters. He enjoyed picnics and shared our joy from his wheelchair. One evening three of us younger Sisters took him to the movie theater in Victoria to see *Oh, God*. We enjoyed hamburgers afterward from the back of his specialized van given to him by the archdiocese. He made that night special for everyone who greeted him, and he for the first time in so many years enjoyed a night out at the movies. Optimism reigned eternal as he pursued his activities every day.

He suffered his passion on earth, as so many times he came close to being martyred due to his illness. One morning the footboard of his rocking bed came loose and he slid to the floor. I rushed to his side and cradled his head in my lap until the fire department men came to lift him and he was able to breathe more easily again. Gentle strength was his every day of his life. I also remember when he developed pneumonia and we had to take him to San Antonio by ambulance. Doctor Ciborowski was in his pick-up truck following the ambulance closely carrying Fr. Kram's rocking bed for him to use in ICU at the hospital.

He had a purpose in life and he knew it. He pursued the priesthood with everything he had every day. He took back some of the control over life that life had so cruelly taken from him so many years prior on the brink of his priesthood. His resilience and serenity, his simplicity, spirituality, and stability made him a saint we all know him to be.

I would take him in his special van to visit his mother in the Shiner nursing home. He was so tender with her. As a son is to his mother, it was a heart-warming sight. On one trip to Shiner, I turned the corner too quickly, and although his wheelchair was secured in his van, it tilted to one side on two wheels. Father C started laughing; I pulled over to be sure he was all right. Of course, he assured me he was fine, but he would tease me about our little trip rather often. I still smile when I think of him.

If we waited until the time was absolutely right, many of us would never get to do what we really wanted to do. Father Kram never let an opportunity pass; he did what he wanted to do, and that was minister to everyone he met, no matter how he was feeling at the time. He truly made a difference for others. He consciously and deliberately lived each and every day with enthusiasm and joy.

The need to belong and the need to be special, these are what he wanted others to feel, and in doing so, I believe he felt that way himself. His attempt to meet these needs for others and himself were intricately woven into all his relationships.

His life was one of heroics. His faith in God and people were exercised every day of his life. He was not able to care for his own needs, and he had faith and trusted that those around him would support him. He was totally dependent on others, and yet he made us all feel that we could not do without him, and we were dependent on him for our needs. I am sure that his living brought back many to the Faith.

His fortitude and courage in the midst of everyday hardships, his steadfast spirit and willingness to do well in spite of all the obstacles were motivating. One cannot imagine how he continued on for so many years in the midst of all the unfamiliar territory that he encountered no matter where he was living. His move from the seclusion of his Shiner home with his parents to the life of living as the chaplain of the old Huth Hospital to moving to the new hospital and getting used to new everyday living was an inspiration to many. His hours in prayer and celebrating Mass were spiritual adventures for those who were privileged to be with him at those times. The little chapel was filled to overflowing. The privilege of assisting him at Mass was a treasured memory. I remember we went to the home of Mr. and Mrs. Frank Raska, Marie Wegener's parents, to celebrate a home Mass for their fiftieth wedding anniversary. What a special occasion that was for all of us.

The priest, to be a priest, must be "taken" from among men—that is, invested somehow with the character of God himself. He must represent God before the people. Such is the honor of the priesthood. It is an honor so lofty that no man may take it to himself; he must be called to the priesthood by God. Father Kram was certainly called and in answering his call, he blessed all of us, who were fortunate to have been a part of his life.

Father Kram was firm in his beliefs; he trusted a God who took care of him for all those years. He never wavered in his love for his church and ministry. He lived his life in the daily routine with a smile and true love for all.

He is a saint; no doubt about it. His heavenly journey began nine years ago when he died. We are all blessed to have known him, to have allowed him to be a part of our lives, and he let so many of us be a part of his. He always found a way to love us and to love the Lord.

The last time I saw him was August 12, 2000, the day before he died. I drove from Houston to spend time with him, as Doctor Ciborowski had emailed that there was not much time left. We spoke about all the old days and as I kissed him farewell, he smiled his special smile so unique to him, and he said we would meet one day in heaven. He had trouble breathing that day, yet he only cared for those who were with him. He smiled in his pain. He was resigned to his being with the Lord very soon. Yet he wanted to live to be of service. His very being was service to all.

In life, he silently suffered and endured pain while serving his flock. In death, his example of sacrifice will remain with us for eternity. I will never ever forget him, a Saint among us.

This remarkable testimony came from Joseph Jakubik who knew Fr. Kram for more than fifty years;

I first met Fr. Kram when I entered high school at St. John's Seminary in San Antonio in September 1948. Contact between major and minor seminarians was strictly limited, but because we were from neighboring parishes at home, I got to know him better than I knew most of the other major seminarians. I had just finished high school (minor seminary) when he was stricken with poliomyelitis. I saw him very few times the following years that he lived on the farm with his parents.

In 1956, I left the seminary and I was living a considerable distance from the area, but I did attend Fr. Kram's ordination and first Mass in December 1975. In 1977 he became the chaplain at Huth Memorial Hospital in Yoakum. My mother lived only about a block from the hospital, so when I came to spend a weekend or longer with her, we would attend Saturday morning Mass in the hospital chapel. After Mass we usually visited with him for a while. In the spring of 1988, I moved back to Yoakum and into my mother's house. I became an Extra-Ordinary Minister of Communion at St. Joseph Church and often assisted Fr. Kram at Mass. This continued until his death in August 2000. I was honored that he had requested that I be one of the pallbearers at his funeral.

Although Fr. Kram, during the time I knew him best, seldom left the confines of the hospital in which he served as chaplain, he was aware that his ministry, through his prayers, the Liturgy of the Hours, and especially through the Mass, extended to all the people of God. He had great respect for the teachings of the Church, for his bishop and for the Bishop of Rome.

There was always a joy about him. He had an uplifting effect on all with whom he came in contact. I never heard him complain about his affliction. Father was aware that despite his infirmity, God had a special mission for him. He accepted his situation without complaint and did not let it diminish his efforts to bring compassion and God's mercy to those to whom he served.

I consider Fr. Kram to be a holy man in that he lived his life to the best of his ability in accordance with his faith in Jesus Christ and the Church. He was not "holy" in the sense of showing outward forms of piety excessively. I felt that his holiness was deeply internal and so strong that it was obvious to those who knew him without him being artificial.

I think he should be canonized as a saint and I believe he will be. He would be a model for those people who are paraplegics and quadriplegics and those who suffer any kind of paralysis. He would also be an excellent example and model for all of us. We all have difficulties or infirmities to overcome. He is already a great inspiration to those who knew him whether they are Catholic or non-Catholic.

His deep devotion to the Blessed Virgin Mary was beautiful and holy.

Another friend of forty-five years gave an interesting story with her recollections. This was from Margaret Mary Loos of Yoakum:

I knew Fr. Kram from the time I was a teenager in 1955 until his death in 2000. As an adult, I assisted him at Mass many times. He was my spiritual advisor most of my life.

He was gentle, compassionate, and friendly, never demanding, always patient and respectful of human life. He had a good sense of humor and he had a fine memory, easily remembering people's names after he met them. He warmly greeted everyone he encountered and he recognized the presence of God in everyone.

He had a firm belief in God. He and I often prayed together and I treasure those joyful times. He often prayed in praise of God and thanked God for his priestly vocation. He often spoke about the beauty of heaven and his desire for the kingdom of God.

I consider him to have been a holy person, always in a close relationship with God. People came to the hospital to attend his Masses and to receive the sacraments from him. He was sought by many for the Sacrament of Reconciliation and the healing power of God's forgiveness. His manner of counseling people touched their hearts and changed their lives.

People recognized him as a "special" priest with an unusual relationship with God. He often prayed for people's personal intentions as those prayers were answered. I can attest to three occasions when God responded favorably to prayers for my intentions and those of my family.

My mother, a diabetic with Parkinson's disease, had a leg and foot with very limited circulation. The foot was cold, hard, blue-black in color. She was in the hospital to have the foot amputated the next morning. During Mass we prayed for her recovery. During the doctor's evening visit to her, he found the leg and foot to be warm and natural-colored. He cancelled the surgery and her recovery was complete. The doctor had no explanation for her changed condition and said he had never seen anything like that before.

My son-in-law had an oil field accident in which a steel particle punctured one of his eyes. After surgery a few days later, his eye began to collapse. The doctor did another procedure that held up for a while, but when the dressing was removed from the eye, the doctor noted that the eyeball had collapsed. He scheduled another surgery for the next day. (Through all these procedures, the doctor cautioned my son-in-law that he would never be able to regain full vision from that eye due to the nature of the injury.) That evening, the evening before the next surgery, Fr. Kram celebrated a special Mass for my son-in-law's intentions with our entire family present praying for God's assistance. The day the doctor removed the bandage, my son-in-law had 20/20 vision in that eye. He healed from the surgical procedure and currently has perfect vision in the injured eye.

I had a large kidney stone that would not pass. My doctor recommended surgical removal and I was admitted to the hospital for that purpose. Due to lung problems that I have, the doctor wouldn't allow me to be put to sleep and I was sent home, suffering with considerable pain. At Mass, I prayed for God's help. I went to Fr. Kram and we prayed together and he anointed me with the Sacrament of the Sick. The next evening I passed the stone without pain and with very little bleeding. The stone was large and jagged. It was a blessing to be free of that matter and I have not had any recurrence since then.

I am convinced that God responded to my needs through the intercession of Fr. Kram's prayers.

Emma Raska knew Fr. Kram for more than twenty years. She remembers him with these thoughts:

Father Kram was my dear friend and my spiritual counselor. I tried to help him with some of his routine chores like sorting his mail or helping him with his Mass schedule, but I could never help him as much as he helped me.

His example of suffering patiently while maintaining a positive cheerful attitude is a true lesson in humility that I try to copy.

I visited with him often and always when I left him, I had such a peaceful feeling from just being with him. He had somewhat of a charisma about him that you would not forget.

His visits with the patients were an inspiration to anyone who was present. It seemed that he always knew just the right time to come into the room and exactly the right things to say. The visits allowed him to offer each patient a blessing that seemed to give them the strength and will to live and get well. I know that's what happened to my father when he was a patient there. The doctor had told me my father would probably not make it through the night. He had a punctured lung resulting from being run over by his own pick-up in a freak accident. Dad bled a lot and he was very weak. Father Kram anointed him with the Sacrament of the Sick.

In spite of the doctor's comment that Dad would not likely make it through the night, Dad recovered and lived another five years.

Mrs. Raska ended her comments with these remarks:

I think Fr. Kram was a living saint. He didn't see his plight the way most of us would, with an earthly vision. He had a strength that was not of this earth. His faith and soul knew no boundaries. Father Kram was a man of truth, a man with the courage of his convictions.

Father Kram's extraordinariness comes from the way he lived his life in a wheelchair, completely dependent on other people, like an infant unable to feed himself without mechanical means, yet he was the sunshine of the hospital by always being pleasant.

He may have had heavenly visitors. I wish now that I would have asked him, but knowing Father as I did, I'm sure he would not have told me if he did. He was such a humble person.

Father was totally resigned to God's holy will and he welcomed it as the fruit is to a tree.

Father Paul O'Sullivan, O.P., said, "To love God is to be a saint, and the more we love God, the greater saints we shall be."

Father Charles loved God and he was loved by God.

I was blessed to have known Fr. Kram. I shall always remember him. I truly believe he is a candidate for canonization.

Monsignor Lawrence Stuebben of San Antonio met Fr. Charles in 1948 when they were both students at St. John's Seminary. They remained friends forever. He recalls Fr. Charles with these thoughts:

He was a direct and straightforward person, a true gentleman with a very good mind and a very helping spirit. His parents were beautiful people and simplicity was one of his great virtues. He was very steadfast in all that he did and he remained joyful throughout the difficult times and conditions of his life.

To be paralyzed from the neck down at an early age in life and continue in that condition for many years without complaint and with optimism, cheerfulness, and zeal was truly an example for all of us. After his ordination, which was a great Witness to God's goodness, he continued to manifest these qualities in his ministry as a hospital chaplain. The very length and constancy of his strong faith, splendid hope, and immense charity was a Witness to many, many people.

I truly witnessed his zeal as he wrote and published articles, stayed in touch with many people as an amateur radio operator, stayed very aware of people and ministries locally, nationally, and internationally. He constantly showed by his life and work the call to build God's kingdom and make God present in our world.

Anyone who knew him was struck by his deep faith, fantastic peace and joy and his readiness to do God's will in whatever way he could. His steadfastness, his perseverance, his joy, his generosity and commitment to serve others were rooted in a very deep relationship with God in a very beautiful, simple, and genuine holiness.

Ann Margaret Kutac gave us this interesting and humorous tribute to her friendship with Fr. Kram:

After Fr. Kram took up residence at the Huth Memorial Hospital, it became a second home to me. I lived just around the corner from the hospital so it was nice to walk over and visit with Father any time I was free from other commitments, to help him with small tasks or to just visit. We enjoyed each other's company so there were always fun things to do. He was always in a happy spirit and loved being with people and, at the same time, ministering to their requests. Many times I would stop in before going to my regular day job or again I would come in the evening when I had more free time to do his requests. The time together would pass so quickly that many times the night nurse would come and tell me the back door was being locked for the night and it was time to say goodnight.

Because of his health conditions, Father's sleeping was at times very difficult, so he lived most of the time in his wheelchair that he could operate himself and move anywhere in the hospital. My special time was the privilege to be his assistant minister whenever he celebrated Mass. That is when we began singing hymns during Mass, even though we did not have an organist. Father knew I could handle the music part and everyone present learned the music and sang, and Father was happy about that. This made his celebration of the Mass complete for him.

One day Father asked me if I would take him in his specially equipped blue van to a celebration party to which he had been invited by a family that lived about six miles west of Yoakum. I gave it some thought and accepted his offer to take him. When I arrived at the hospital for the trip, the van was in place, prepared for his ride. The nurses kindly and gently slipped Fr. Kram into the back of the van and I slid into the driver's seat. I had to mentally prepare myself for this trip as I was being entrusted with taking care of God's precious gift, the one and only Fr. Kram. He immediately became my backseat driver and I was happy for that. He instructed me how to drive down the ramp on the emergency lane and how to turn the corners without spilling him into the windows of the van. You must remember he had to lie flat on his back with only the ceiling to stare at because he could not move his head in any way. Do we healthy people ever count how many times we move our body in any direction and Father never could and never complained, so to live this kind of life, is that a saint or what?

Once we moved on down the streets of Yoakum, I started to ramble about what was on the yards and Father promptly reminded me that he could not turn to see what I was seeing and he told me to describe what I saw so he could imagine what I was talking about. When we drove along the highway and I saw late grazing cows in the pastures or birds flying to the woods for the night, it hurt my soul that Father could not see but could only imagine, from my description, the beauty of God's creation that we take so much for granted, and here was this special person who humbled me to be forever grateful to God.

When we arrived at the celebration party, loving hands quickly helped take Father from the back of the van and set him in his special wheelchair. Wow! Was he ever excited! All those people plus music and food and, of course, the Czech and German people make their fellowship with some ice-cold beer. I fed Father his meal, letting him enjoy all that food to his heart's desire.

Before we realized it, the nine o'clock hour was upon us and we knew we had to get back to the hospital before the back door was locked for the night. We expressed our appreciation for the evening of fun and began our return to town. The loving angels put Father into the van, and he and I headed back to Yoakum. On the way back, I described to Father the beautiful star-lit night. It had been a beautiful summer evening, and I know his head and heart were bursting with happy memories. As I recall that evening, I know that God had done everything perfect for the two of us that day. When we arrived at the back door of the hospital, the nurses were waiting for us and they teased Father about staying out so late on his date. They lovingly removed him from the van and once more returned him to his home, left to daydream about the fun he had.

My family and I were in Port Aransas for the weekend when God called Fr. Kram home to himself. Father had been sick off and on but I didn't realize that his lifetime was about to end. God had spared me the pain of seeing his passing from this life to eternity, but each day when I pass the old hospital, I can see Father's room and I remember all the love he gave to everyone that passed through those doors.

I can't even begin to imagine the joy of Fr. Kram when God said to him, "Come, faithful servant, to share your Creator's joy forever," and Father stood up and walked into the arms of God leaving behind forever the wheelchair and all that it represented.

Living life is about human relationships, not material possessions. I will always cherish the friendship of Fr. Kram.

Here is another interesting story for us. It comes from Mrs. Marie O. Gomez whom Father knew simply as "Yellow Rose":

Early one beautiful spring morning in October of 1988, my cousin, Rubye Hermes, and I drove to Yoakum, Texas, 150 miles from our home in San Antonio. We were going to attend a memorial Mass for Lucy Hermes, wife of Patrick Hermes and mother of Edward, Buddy, and Alton Hermes of Ezzell. The Mass was to be celebrated in Huth Memorial Hospital Chapel there in Yoakum.

Since we arrived early, we entered the chapel to prepare for Mass before the celebrant's arrival. After kneeling and reciting several Hail Marys, I sat down to continue praying. While I was seated, I turned and saw a gentleman whose wheelchair was being placed in the aisle beside my pew by a Sister dressed in white. I presumed she was a nurse bringing in the patient to attend Mass. I again turned my head and was in awe when I saw the patient's arms extended and supported on what appeared to be two gauze padded boards. Not wanting to stare, I again looked straight ahead. Only a few minutes passed and my curiosity got the best of me and I nonchalantly turned to look at the wheelchair patient again. I couldn't help but see that he even had a tracheotomy. I also noticed his very thin legs under the clinging lap throw. After observing the gentleman's heartbreaking medical condition, I thought to myself how very fortunate I was to be able to breathe, move my extremities, and function normally. I quickly said a silent prayer for God to help that poor patient cope with his infirmities.

About five more minutes passed and I saw the same Sister pushing the wheelchair down the aisle of the chapel straight to the front of the altar and then turning to go behind it. *Dear God*, I wondered, *where is that Sister taking that poor patient now?*

Ten minutes later I was extremely surprised upon seeing that same wheelchair patient garbed in priest vestments. I also saw when his chair was pushed right up against the altar. I presumed the Sister remained to the left of the priest to be ready to assist him when necessary.

Needless to say, I was moved to tears when I first heard that priest begin to speak in a very cheerful voice.

"Good morning everyone. I am Fr. Charles Kram, and I welcome you to our chapel on this beautiful morning. I want to thank you for attending this memorial Mass for Mrs. Lucy Hermes that I will be privileged to celebrate," etc., etc., etc.

I don't believe there were many dry eyes in the chapel as Fr. Charles Kram began the Mass. What a moving and impressive sight for us to behold.

Attending that Mass celebrated by Fr. Kram, a totally dependent quadriplegic, was the turning point in my life. Having had seven children, my husband and I were being kept quite busy caring for them. I should also add that I was a diabetic checking my blood sugar four to five times a day and injecting insulin according to a sliding scale. So be assured that at the particular time my morale was quite low—that being the understatement of the year.

Father Kram's warm words of welcome, his obvious inner strength, fortitude, perseverance, and visible devotion to his vocation served as a miraculous tonic for me. I thought that if this dear priest carries on so patiently, so devoutly, and so pleasantly, I surely can and will begin to carry my light cross without complaining.

Upon my return home, I hurriedly penned a letter of end-less thanks and praise to Fr. Kram. I explained that after attending his beautiful Mass, hearing his positive words, and observing his holiness, I promised God and his Blessed Mother to change my life around and to strive to do better.

In my letter, I also described one of my typical days and asked him to please occasionally remember my family in his prayers. As I was about to end my incoherent epistle, I decided to inject a little humor. I signed off by using the name of "Yellow Rose" and never divulging my real name.

About a week passed and I was pleasantly surprised to receive a letter addressed to "Yellow Rose" at my address. (Much later I was informed that Father had to hold a stick in his mouth to type letters on his computer.) Can you imagine that difficult, tedious task?

Father's letters were always short but interesting and very inspiring. His examples of perseverance and love for Christ always served as great encouragements. In spite of his dis-comfort and suffering, his sense of humor was always like a ray of sunshine entering some of my dreary days. I felt blessed to receive Father's letters for many years.

Years later, when our children were old enough, my hus-band and I decided we could take a break and enjoy a tour of Europe. I was fortunate to meet a lovely lady in our group from Yoakum, Texas. I immediately asked her if she knew Fr. Kram. After she replied in the affirmative, I inquired if she had ever heard Fr. Kram mention "Yellow Rose."

"Oh yes," she answered, "I believe he pictures her to be a young lady with red hair." "And probably with freckles," I added, while laughing to myself. But, oh how very wrong that guess would be, for I am an older Spanish lady with jet-black hair.

I could make this letter longer and easily ramble on, but I will spare you, dear patient readers, from getting irritated eyes.

Yes, I did visit Fr. Kram several times, and yes, I eventually confessed to him that I was Yellow Rose, and yes, he has been the most influential person in my life, and yes, to this day I ask him to intercede for my family and friends, and yes, my fervent prayers are for Fr. Charles Kram to be beatified and then eventually canonized, for he is truly deserving of that crowning glory. In my estimation, he is already a saint.

Sincerely meant, Fr. Kram's friend "Yellow Rose,"
Mrs. Maria O. Gomez.

What a glorious testimony that is!
Sister Frances Cabrini told this beautiful story about Fr. Charles:

I think the Sisters at St. Ludmila Academy prayed Fr. Charles into ordination because I was a young Sister when I went to Shiner, and I used to drive some of the older Sisters out to visit his mother and father and him at their farm before his ordination. He would draw cartoons with a pencil in his mouth and he showed us how he operated his radio. He was very connected with the Sisters in Shiner and, as I said, they prayed him through a lot of crises, like when his mother died and when his father died. I remember him at the altar in his wheelchair celebrating the funeral Mass for his father and what a traumatic experience that death was for him. The loss of his father when his mother was in the nursing home was a real blow to him. Yet he had faith in the providence of God and knew that God comes to the aid of those who love him. Through the efforts of many people, he was assigned to the hospital in Yoakum as Hospital Chaplain. He fit right into that role as if he had been made for it. It was not unusual for some people to think they were terribly bad off with whatever hardships they had until they saw Fr. Charles coming down the hall guiding his wheelchair with his chin. He would lift their spirits even if his own were down. He was a person that knew how to manage people's emotions and needs. He even did a great job of managing his own emotions because, you can imagine, he was a person so limited in what he could do. Yet he was able to do so many things so well.

For example, there was a Sister with us who was from Mexico. She was Sister Anna Luna. She wanted to go to confession but she didn't speak English very well. Father understood enough Spanish that he could hear her confession. She told us afterward that she told him that she was scheduled to go to Kenya to do missionary work, but she was afraid to go because she had a hard time with the English language that is spoken there. She said Fr. Charles told her not to worry because she had a beautiful smile and the smile is a universal language. And so, she was relieved of her anxieties. She went to Kenya remembering his kind assurances that the smile is a universal language.

Sister Frances simply marveled at his ability to say the right things at the right moment.

Janet Pohl wrote this summary of Fr. Kram's life for the August 14, 2000, edition of the *YCH Partners Update*, the official publication of the Yoakum Community Hospital:

A Tribute to Father Kram (09/29/1929 to 08/13/2000)

Father Kram was always there with a smile and a joke. He always knew just what to say to brighten the day. Color and religion did not stop him from praying with all and being there for the sick. He was always giving of himself and always trying to make things right. His disabilities did not stop him. He was a whiz on the computer and was always inventing something to make things more accessible to him so he could be more independent. As space got smaller at the new hospital, he didn't complain, he just kept packing them in to the Chapel Sunday after Sunday. Seeing Father Kram with the strength that came from his positive attitude made others stronger and able to go on.

It was always so amazing that he was at our mercy to do things for him, yet he never complained when we were too busy—he would always say, "When you have time." Father bought raffle tickets from local charities and the EMS and would have me write in others' names, saying, "After all, what would I need that stuff for?" He gave unselfishly when it was convenient for others and not for him.

The hospital will surely be lonelier now knowing that we'll never hear the sound of his wheelchair coming down the hall or around the next corner. He has truly touched our lives and so many more that we don't even know about. Padre, you were one of a kind.

A later edition (January 1, 2001) of *YCH Partners Update* included an information item by Jeff R. Egbert concerning a substantial money donation the hospital received from Fr. Kram's estate. It was reported that the money would be used for the acquisition and installation of the HMS Computer Information System, a project in which Fr. Kram had been very interested. The hospital family was grateful for his support and generous gift.

The August 13, 2001, edition of the hospital publication observed the first anniversary of Fr. Kram's death with this remembrance by an anonymous poet:

In Remembrance

Father Charles W. Kram, Jr.

Ordained: December 5, 1975—Died August 13, 2000

> *Don't think of him as gone away,*
> > *His journey's just begun.*
> *Life holds so many facets,*
> > *This earth is only one.*
> *Just think of him as resting*
> > *From the sorrows and the tears,*
> > *In a place of warmth and comfort*
> > *Where there are no days and years.*
> *Think how he must be wishing*
> > *That he could know today*
> > *How nothing but our sadness*
> > *Can really pass away.*
> *And think of him as living*
> > *In the hearts of those he touched,*
> > *For nothing loved is ever lost*
> > *And he was loved so much.*

Father Charles W. Kram, Jr.

CHAPTER SIXTEEN

Is Sainthood Possible?

His Master said to him, "Well done, my good and faithful servant. Since you were faithful in small matters, I will give you great responsibilities. Come, share your master's joys." (Matthew 25:21)

Strictly speaking, for someone to be declared by the Church to be a saint, permitting public veneration by the faithful, the life of the person must be carefully and thoroughly scrutinized to ascertain that the person lived a holy life and presently shares in the face-to-face presence of God.

The Church teaches that holiness of life and heroic virtue mark someone a saint. The doctrine of the communion of saints confirms the belief that Christians are united together in life and death. It is how we live that reveals the measure of our holiness, and, therefore, our place in eternity.

Practically speaking, it is reasonable to believe that everyone who is in heaven is a saint whether or not the Church has declared them to be a saint.

Throughout this biography, we have heard from people who knew Fr. Charles Kram. We know and believe that it is God who is the sole judge of our holiness. But here is what some of his cheering section have to say in Fr. Kram's behalf.

John Butschek gave these comments: "Father Kram lived forty-seven years with his infirmities, administering to people of many faiths and even to some with no faith. He never wavered in his love, devotion, and purpose of his own faith. What satisfaction our Lord must see in him. As an *Alter Christus*, would not these words be appropriate? 'This is my beloved son in whom I am well pleased.'"

Phyllis Lauer said, "I have never known another person like Fr. Kram. I admired him greatly. He was a mentor to me. I feel so blessed to have had him in my life. I am a better person because of him. In my eyes, he was/is a saint."

Emma Raska, who knew Fr. Kram for more than twenty years, said, "I think he is a saint. He didn't see his plight the way most of us would—with an earthly vision. He had a strength that was not of this earth. His faith and soul knew no limits. He was a man of truth, a man with the courage of his convictions."

Mary Butschek was convinced he should be declared a saint. She believed he lived such a heroic life that he would be a perfect patron of the handicapped. He would be an inspiration to everyone suffering difficulties in their lives. She believed that the story of how his faith in God helped him live such a holy and happy life would help others in similar circumstances.

Anne Marie Germani offered this assessment of his worthiness of sainthood:

> He freely chose to divest himself of things and of self. He became the lamb of God. He gave himself and unconditionally to the love of God. His vocation was love and love was his life. God walks among us every day, yet so many times we fail to recognize him in those closest to us.

> It has been written by an unknown author: "The priest, to be a priest, must be taken from among men, that is, he must be a man not different from other men, nor a stranger to them, but identified with them, a sharer in their common human experience; for it is on behalf of mankind that he enters the sanctuary, to represent mankind before God. Such is the lowliness of the priesthood; it is lowliness so profound that no man would wish it for himself. To it, too, God must call him."

> God called Fr. Kram. He gave himself back to God with every labored breath, with every heartbeat until his final *amen*.

Sister M. Sylvia Grahmann, IWBS, was close to Fr. Kram for twenty-nine years. She offered these thoughts:

> Father Kram practiced the works of mercy in many ways, especially as chaplain in the hospital. He visited the sick, anointed patients who were dying or near death, prayed with and for the people, counseled them, heard confessions, celebrated the Mass, preached the gospel, and touched the lives of countless people in his gentle loving manner. He was a holy man, reminding us of the suffering Christ.
>
> I definitely think Fr. Kram should be canonized a saint because he lived his life in an extraordinary way in spite of the many obstacles that crossed his path. His simplicity and humility are extraordinary. Submission to the will of God was evident throughout his life.

There are many more who have testified to Fr. Kram's worthiness of sainthood, but we will wrap it up with these thoughts from Monsignor Lawrence J. Stuebben:

> I have a group of "intercessors" in heaven to whom I speak asking them to intercede for me and those for whom I pray and the needs of our world and Church. They are my personal saints in heaven. They include members of my family and people to whom and with whom I have ministered over the years of my priesthood. Father Charles Kram has been a member of that group since he went home to God. In my mind and faith, he is already a saint in heaven. His life is the kind of example that speaks wonderfully of God's power working in the lives of human beings. In 1952, Charles Kram was preparing for a day in priesthood. As a result of polio, he was paralyzed from the neck down. With much struggle, he remained alive. He was truly alive in every way; spiritually, relationally with God and with people, by the example of his life, he struggled with his illness for many, many years. After a long wait (more than twenty years), he was ordained and then allowed by God to serve in ministry for another quarter of a century. What a

life! It is the kind of journey that inspires others and gives strength and hope to those who need it. My prayers are with all who work with the cause which could be such a blessing to God's people.

Father Charles W. Kram, Jr., spent forty-seven of his seventy years on earth as a quadriplegic and was totally dependent on those around him, but his greatest joy was being able to help everyone he could as his way to give glory to God.

If you have any problems, you might ask Fr. Kram to help you seek and know the will of God for you.

If you are blessed to have had a special relationship or have received any favors from Fr. Kram, please relate the circumstances of those actions to:

FATHER CHARLES KRAM PROJECT
C/O STS. CYRIL & METHODIUS CATHOLIC CHURCH
306 S. AVENUE F
SHINER, TX 77984-8208

Telephone: 361-594-3836
Fax: 361-594-2850

Prayer for the beatification of Fr. Charles Kram:

Dear Father in heaven, we beseech you on behalf of your priest, Fr. Charles Kram, who left us a wonderful example of pastoral charity and patient suffering. If it be your will, grant that he may be numbered among the Blessed in heaven. We ask this through Christ our Lord. Amen.

(Prayer by permission of the Most Reverend David E. Fellhauer, Bishop of the Diocese of Victoria in Texas.)

Epilogue

We have been on a journey through the life of a remarkable man, Charles William Kram, Jr., and the remarkable people around him. We might be tempted to think this is the complete story of his life, but let's be realistic. We have only scratched the surface. It is reasonable to say that for every incident and for every comment and for every act of love recorded in this book, there must be a thousand, or maybe ten thousand, that could be or should be told.

While we are reflecting on all the heroic acts of love of God and neighbor displayed by the primary character of the story, let us not overlook the tremendous acts of love performed by all the people who cared for Fr. Kram. When we realize he spent forty-seven years in a totally helpless condition, dependent on help from other people every minute of every day and night, we are struck with an unbelievable series of Christ-like activities.

The ultimate question that comes to mind is this:

Who was more Christ-like?

Was it Fr. Charles Kram or was it every one of his caregivers?

Perhaps his greatest contribution to the people of his area is that he presented to them many opportunities for them to display their remarkable capacity of love.

It is fitting that we thank God for placing in our midst the remarkable Fr. Kram *and* the remarkable people who took care of him. All of them together are an outstanding example to us of the opportunities that God gives to us to exercise our willingness to express the love that Jesus meant when he spoke of the greatest commandments: "You shall love the Lord, your God, with all your heart, with all your soul, and with all your mind. This is the greatest and first commandment. The second is like it: you shall love your neighbor as yourself. The whole law and the prophets depend on these two commandments" (Matthew 22:37–40).

May God richly reward them all. Amen.

Acknowledgments

Deo Gratias

Thanks be to God who gives us victory through our Lord Jesus Christ. (1 Corinthians 15:57)

No matter how we turn the crank or spin the dial for the proper words to say, the first and most important expression of gratitude is always: "Thanks be to God for all the graces, for all the gifts, for all the patience, for all the love, for all the guidance and inspiration, and for all the humility that are needed to produce a work of this nature."

Without all the help we received from God, there would be no story to tell, nor anyone to write it, nor anyone to read it. God's hand is found in all we think and do and say, and for that we are grateful.

Next, we thank Fr. Charles William Kram, Jr., and all the participants in this story for living the lives they lived so there would be a story to tell.

We acknowledge with deep gratitude the important roles in this endeavor exercised by Fr. Robert E. Knippenberg and the late Mary Butschek. They began the process of assembling information and documenting critical testimony regarding the life of Fr. Kram. Father Bob opened the doors of Church Records and provided the guidelines to follow in consideration of Fr. Kram's worthiness to be eventually "raised to our altars." While Fr. Bob was performing this service, Mary Butschek was organizing Father Kram's writings and homilies and initiating the assembly of testimony from close associates and family and friends regarding Fr. Kram's life. It was an enormous task that she undertook, and her contribution toward the success of this project cannot be measured.

The five-person committee that took up the challenge when Fr. Bob was moved to another parish in the diocese and Mary Butschek passed into eternity has exhibited an enormous capacity for work and love of God in the process of gathering and preserving more information on the life of Fr. Kram. This committee is chaired by Deacon Joe Machacek who is the Business Manager of Sts. Cyril and Methodius Church. Other vital members of that committee are John Butschek (close friend of Fr. Kram and husband of the late Mary Butschek), Hazel Pfeil (retired nurse who knew Fr. Kram since their childhood and who cared for him in the hospital from 1977 to his death in 2000), and Karen Roznovsky and her sister Janet Pohl (who both knew Fr. Kram from their childhood and were both employed at the hospital in Yoakum). These loving and caring persons all had intimate knowledge of the life and ministry of Fr. Kram and their reflections on his life are included in the story. This group solicited my help to write this biography following the recommendation of Fr. Kirby Hlavaty, pastor of Sts. Cyril and Methodius Church, who knew me from when he was pastor of St. Michael Church in Cuero. This committee of five made available to me all the information they had on Fr. Kram's life, and they generously contributed their wisdom and support throughout the writing of this book. They also acted as local editors of my manuscript and made invaluable contributions to its completion. To them, I am very grateful.

Finally, next to God in strength of support to me in this project and all the endeavors of my life is my wife, Dawn. Without her love and support and encouragement, this project would not exist. In addition, she served as my proofreader searching for grammar and punctuation errors that no writer can find in his own work. I cannot find the words to adequately express my total appreciation, except to simply say, "Thank you, dear, for this and all your help over the past sixty-plus years of our marriage."

To all of these beautiful helpers, I am deeply indebted.

For all of you I say, "Thanks be to God."

Author's Profile

In 1988 Anthony Warzecha, known by his relatives and friends as Tony, retired from active employment after thirty-four years in the automobile finance business, which followed three years in the army during the Korea Conflict of the 1950s. In 1996, at the age of sixty-five, he answered God's call to enter into the five-year formation program for ordination as a permanent deacon for the Diocese of Victoria in Texas. In 2001 he was ordained a deacon at the age of seventy and was assigned to serve the Catholic Community of Cuero, Texas.

Early in 2012 at the age of eighty, he resigned from active parish ministry to devote his attention to retirement activities. The release from active parish ministries enabled him to finish writing a book about his parents and the family they raised.

That book, *The Warzechas of Mustang Mott*, was published by Trafford Publishing Company of Bloomington, Indiana, in time for distribution to attendees at the Warzecha Family Reunion in 2012. Its success and his successful ministry titled "Ask the Deacon," answering questions about our faith and Catholic worship and customs from the faithful in the community as an insert into the weekly bulletins of the two parishes in his town led to an invitation from Sts. Cyril and Methodius Catholic Church in Shiner, Texas, to write the biography of Fr. Charles W. Kram, Jr.

A committee of five individuals dedicated to preserving the memory and documenting the life of Fr. Kram had been gathering information and collecting testimony on Fr. Kram's life since soon after his death.

This book is drawn from those archives plus additional interviews and investigations made by the author.

The author is married to Dawn, and they have two sons and daughters-in-law and one grandson in college. He and his wife are active at St. Michael Church and local community affairs, including the Veterans of Foreign Wars of which both they and their sons are life members, all having served our country in times and places of imminent danger; they are, however, peaceful by nature and prefer peaceful settlements of all conflicts. For more than twenty years, he and Dawn have provided the local military honors ceremony at the burial of honorably discharged veterans.

He is an accomplished stained glass artist, having enjoyed the art as a hobbyist who occasionally did commissioned works. He reads a lot, mostly Catholic literature. He enjoyed outdoor activities until his age slowed down such efforts. Quiet time indoors doing word games with Dawn is his current favorite activity.

His recent interest in writing has taken him into a new role and he does not rule out the prospect of writing another book.

Index

About Leonine Publishers

Leonine Publishers LLC makes fine Catholic literature available to Catholics throughout the English-speaking world. Leonine Publishers offers an innovative "hybrid" approach to book publication that helps authors as well as readers. Please visit our web site at www.leoninepublishers.com to learn more about us. Browse our online bookstore to find more solid Catholic titles to uplift, challenge, and inspire.

Our patron and namesake is Pope Leo XIII, a prudent, yet uncompromising pope during the stormy years at the close of the 19th century. Please join us as we ask his intercession for our family of readers and authors.

Do you have a book inside you? Visit our web site today. Leonine Publishers accepts manuscripts from Catholic authors like you. If your book is selected for publication, you will have an active part in the production process. This book is an example of our growing selection of literature for the busy Catholic reader of the 21st century.

www.leoninepublishers.com

www.ingramcontent.com/pod-product-compliance
Lightning Source LLC
LaVergne TN
LVHW011346080426
835511LV00005B/143